Parenting
TEENAGERS
Systematic Training for Effective Parenting of Teens

Don Dinkmeyer, Sr.
Gary D. McKay
Joyce L. McKay
Don Dinkmeyer, Jr.

American Guidance Service, Inc.
Circle Pines, Minnesota 55014-1796
1-800-328-2560

To all the parents and leaders of STEP/Teen, and to Rudolf Dreikurs—our teacher, friend, and source of encouragement.

Together, we are meeting our responsibility and challenge: Parent education is the right of every teen.

Chapter 1: Problem ownership is from Thomas Gordon, *P.E.T.: Parent Effectiveness Training* (New York: NAL-Dutton, 1975); some information on how teens are changing physically, emotionally, and mentally is from Jane Bluestein, *Parents, Teen, and Boundaries: How to Draw the Line* (Deerfield Beach, FL: Health Communications, 1993) and David Elkind, *Parenting Your Teenager* (New York: Ballantine, 1993); the four goals of misbehavior originated in Rudolf Dreikurs and Vickie Soltz, *Children: The Challenge* (New York: Dutton, 1987); ideas about the goals of excitement, peer pressure, and superiority come from Eugene Kelly and Thomas Sweeney, "Typical Faulty Goals of Adolescents: A Base for Counseling," in *The School Counselor* (March 1979).

Chapter 2: Stepsibling information is from Don Dinkmeyer and Gary D. McKay, *Raising a Responsible Child, Revised* (New York: Fireside, 1996); some of the ideas in "Changing Your Self-Talk" come from Gary D. McKay and Don Dinkmeyer, *How You Feel Is Up to You* (San Luis Obispo, CA: Impact, 1994) and Albert Ellis, *How to Stubbornly Refuse to Make Yourself Miserable About Anything—Yes, Anything!* (Secaucus, NJ: Lyle Stuart, 1988).

Chapter 3: I-messages come from Thomas Gordon, *P.E.T.: Parent Effectiveness Training* (New York: NAL-Dutton, 1975); some ideas on trust come from Jane Bluestein, *Parents, Teen, and Boundaries: How to Draw the Line* (Deerfield Beach, FL: Health Communications, 1993); focusing on strengths and efforts and the "Humor Helps!" activity come Don Dinkmeyer and Lewis L. Losoncy, *The Skills of Encouragement* (Delray Beach, FL: St. Lucie's Press, 1996); the concept of the courage to be imperfect comes from Rudolf Dreikurs.

Chapter 4: Problem-solving steps originated with Rudolf Dreikurs and Loren Grey, *A Parent's Guide to Child Discipline* (New York: Hawthorn, 1970); the job jar is from Don Dinkmeyer and Gary D. McKay, *Raising a Responsible Child, Revised* (New York: Fireside, 1996); ideas on single-parent families and stepfamilies are from Don Dinkmeyer, Gary D. McKay, and Joyce L. McKay, *New Beginnings* (Champaign, IL: Research Press, 1987).

Chapter 6: Some information on schoolwork and logical consequences comes from Don Dinkmeyer and Gary D. McKay, *Raising a Responsible Child, Revised* (New York: Fireside, 1996); some information on depression and suicide comes from the National Institutes of Health (NIH) and Mary Griffin, "Cries for Help," *Guideposts* (July 1980); information on body image and eating disorders comes from Jane Nelson and Lynn Lott, *I'm on Your Side* (Rocklin, CA: Prima Publishing, 1990) and Jane Nelson, Lynn Lott, and H. Stephen Glenn, *Positive Discipline A-Z* (Rocklin, CA: Prima, 1993); information and ideas on gangs come from Don Dinkmeyer and Gary D. McKay, *Raising a Responsible Child, Revised* (New York: Fireside, 1996) and and David Elkind, *Parenting Your Teenager* (New York: Ballantine, 1993); "I noticed" statements come from Jane Nelson, Lynn Lott, and H. Stephen Glenn, *Positive Discipline A-Z* (Rocklin, CA: Prima, 1993).

Chapter 7: Information about legal challenges involving teen fathers' rights is from Don Dinkmeyer and Gary D. McKay, *Raising a Responsible Child, Revised* (New York: Fireside, 1996); information and ideas on alcohol and other drugs come from Gary D. McKay, Joyce L. McKay, and Don Dinkmeyer, *STEP for Substance Abuse Prevention* (Circle Pines, MN: American Guidance Service, 1990) and from the National Institutes of Health (NIH).

Photo Credits: Cover: Steve McHugh, The Photography Group; Chapters 1-3: James L. Schaffer; Chapters 4-7: Cheryl Walsh Bellville.

Matt Keller, *Marketing Director;* Mary Kaye Kuzma, *Purchasing Agent;* Charles Pederson, *Associate Editor;* Teri Mathews, *Senior Editor;* Marjorie Lisovskis, *Writer/Editor;* Evans McCormick Creative, *Design/Typesetting;* John Bush, *Cartoons*

Printed in the United States of America

ISBN 0-7854-1468-1

Product Number 12752

A 0 9 8 7 6 5 4 3 2

Contents

Other Works by the Authors

The Effective Parent (Don Dinkmeyer, Gary D. McKay, Don Dinkmeyer, Jr., James S. Dinkmeyer, and Joyce L. McKay)

The Parent's Handbook (Don Dinkmeyer, Sr., Gary D. McKay, and Don Dinkmeyer, Jr.)

Parenting Young Children: Systematic Training for Effective Parenting of Children Under Six (Don Dinkmeyer, Sr., Gary D. McKay, James S. Dinkmeyer, Don Dinkmeyer, Jr., and Joyce L. McKay)

Systematic Training for Effective Teaching (STET) (Don Dinkmeyer, Sr., Gary D. McKay, and Don Dinkmeyer, Jr.)

Preparing Responsible and Effective Parents (PREP) (Don Dinkmeyer, Sr., Gary D. McKay, Don Dinkmeyer, Jr., James S. Dinkmeyer, and Jon Carlson)

Time for a Better Marriage (Don Dinkmeyer and Jon Carlson)

Raising a Responsible Child: How to Prepare Your Child for Today's Complex World (Revised 1996) (Don Dinkmeyer and Gary D. McKay)

Taking Time for Love: How to Stay Happily Married (Don Dinkmeyer and Jon Carlson)

The Encouragement Book (Don Dinkmeyer and Lewis E. Losoncy)

Leadership by Encouragement (Don Dinkmeyer and Daniel Eckstein)

The Skills of Encouragement (Don Dinkmeyer and Lewis E. Losoncy)

How You Feel Is Up to You: The Power of Emotional Choice (Gary D. McKay and Don Dinkmeyer)

Consultaton in the Schools (Don Dinkmeyer, Jr., Jon Carlson, and Don Dinkmeyer, Sr.)

New Beginnings (Don Dinkmeyer, Sr., Gary D. McKay, and Joyce L. McKay)

Introduction

Being the parent of a teen is rewarding, exciting, and challenging. In making the change from parenting a child to parenting a young adult, you might feel sad as you see your son or daughter leave childhood. Maybe you worry about sex, drugs, violence, eating habits, grades, or friends. Seeing your teen's changing values, you may panic. You might also enjoy watching your teenager grow and mature. Many parents find great satisfaction in "getting to know" the new person who is their gradually maturing teen.

We believe that the rewards of parenting teenagers can far outweigh the challenges. With skills and understanding, you can guide your teen to be responsible, cooperative, and independent. In doing this, you build a strong, positive relationship with your teenager. Even parents facing serious problems with teens can find more effective ways to get along with and help their teenager.

Parenting Teenagers provides a practical approach to help you do this. Millions of parents have found the skills and ideas in this book to be effective. If you put them into practice, they will help you improve your relationship with your teenager. They will help you be the best parent you can be.

Many parents find the teen years the most trying times of all. Some think they've failed in the job of child rearing. Many of these parents also believe that because their teens are practically adults, parents can't influence them or improve family relationships. We believe that parents can develop rewarding relationships with their teenagers and can help their teens become more cooperative, contributing members of the family. Begin by taking reasonable steps with your teens.

We suggest that you pace yourself by spending a week on each chapter. Read each chapter in the order presented. During that week, study the activities and charts in the chapter. Be sure to take time to carry out the activities titled "This Week," "Just for You," and "For Your Family." If you're willing to stick with it, *Parenting Teenagers* will help you take your next good steps as a parent. The skills you learn can serve as guidelines in building a happy home.

Don Dinkmeyer, Sr., Ph.D., Diplomate in Counseling Psychology, American Board of Professional Psychology; Diplomate, American Board of Family Psychology; Clinical Member, American Association for Marriage and Family Therapy

Gary D. McKay, Ph.D., Licensed Psychologist; Clinical Member, American Association for Marriage and Family Therapy

Joyce L. McKay, Ph.D., Certified Professional Counselor

Don Dinkmeyer, Jr., Ph.D., Western Kentucky University; Licensed Marriage and Family Therapist

CHAPTER ONE

Understanding **Yourself** *and* **Your Teenager**

Mom walks in the door after work Friday. Fifteen-year-old Tony greets her at the door. He says, "After the game tonight, I'm going to a party at Paul's." Mom sets down a bag of groceries and asks, "Who's Paul?" Tony sighs impatiently, "A guy from school—he's a junior. I'm gonna eat at Mike's before the game. I need you to drive me over there."

"Wait a minute," says Mom. "I just walked in the door. We need to talk about this." Angry, Tony raises his voice and says, "Mom, I've gotta go now. I promised Mike I'd be there by six. If we're late for the game, it'll be my fault!" Mom tries to stay calm. "Does Mike's mom know you're coming for supper? How will you get to the game?" Tony rolls his eyes and says, "We're gonna take the bus from Mike's. Then we'll get a ride from Paul to his place." "Will Paul's parents be home?" asks Mom. "Mom!" says Tony. "It's his dad's apartment—and he'll be home!"

Mom says, "I think I'd better talk to Paul's dad about this." "Mom!" shouts Tony angrily, "I told you he'd be home! Don't embarrass me by calling him! Why you don't trust me?" Mom starts to answer, "Tony, of course I trust you. It's just—" Tony interrupts, "Can you give me a ride to Mike's, or not?" Mom says, "Tony, I need to know more about your plans." Tony yells, "Why are you doing this to me? Nobody else's parents make such a big deal over a game and a party!" He runs to the bedroom and slams the door.

Mom closes her eyes and sighs. She wonders to herself, "Where did that happy little boy go who was so eager to please?"

Here's what you will learn . . .

- Your parenting challenge is to help your teenager be confident, responsible, and independent.

- You help your teen by working to improve your relationship.

- Respect is important for a positive relationship.

- Your teenager's behavior has a purpose.

As a parent of a teenager, you probably know how this parent feels. The child who once cooperated now rebels and speaks rudely. The child who once enjoyed the family now has time only for friends. You might ask, "Why is this happening? How can I make my teenager respect me and cooperate? Is it too late?"

It's Not Too Late

Your teen is no longer a child—and not yet an adult. Neither of you can go back in time. Is it too late to help your teenager grow more confident, responsible, and cooperative? No.

Many parents want to "fix" the problems they have with their children. The truth is that you *can't* fix your teenager. You can't *make* your teenager do anything. What you *can* do is work on your relationship with your teenager. You can start to build a positive atmosphere for dealing with problems. You can change the way you communicate. As you begin to change your approach, your relationship with your teenager is likely to start to change as well.

It's not too late. But change must start with you. You are the only person you can change.

Parenting Skills Can Be Learned

Being a parent takes skill. You can learn, practice, and improve your parenting skills. You can learn to:

- Treat your teen—and yourself—with respect.
- Understand the goals of misbehavior and change the way you respond.
- Become skilled at encouraging your teen.
- Listen to your teen's feelings.
- Express your own feelings so your teen is more willing to listen to you.
- Encourage your teen to make decisions and learn from them.
- Discipline in positive, effective ways.

Parenting Teenagers can guide you to meet your parenting challenges. It can help you find ways to build a better relationship with your teenager, one step at a time. Follow the steps in order. Practice what they teach. As you do, your skills and your confidence in yourself will grow.

You can't make your teenager change. You can change your relationship with your teen.

As you work on the skills, keep your parenting challenge in mind:

- **to encourage your teenager to be healthy, confident, and cooperative**
- **to build a strong, lifelong relationship with your teenager**
- **to help your teenager grow to be a responsible adult**

What Style of Parenting Will Help Me Meet My Goal?

The way you relate to your teenager is your *parenting style*. There are many styles of parenting. The three most common are giving orders, giving in, and giving choices.

Few people follow one style to the extreme. But each of us uses one approach more than the others. As you read, think about your own parenting style. Ask yourself:

- How will my style help me meet the challenge of parenting?
- What can I change to help me and my teen?

Giving Orders

Some parents think teenagers can be forced to obey. These parents think family life will improve if they "get tough" and make sure teens follow their orders. Sometimes the parents yell or hit. This style of parenting is often called *authoritarian*. Parents who use this style tend to criticize their teenagers. They demand and threaten. They use punishment or rewards to control. They remind and nag. They get too involved in homework. They don't trust or respect their teens.

What Do Teens Learn?

When a parent gives orders, teens respond in different ways. Some get angry and rebel in areas we can't control—like friends, smoking, school, drugs, or sex. Then the parent and teen have a power struggle. One or the other may "win" for a while. But respect is lost. The relationship suffers.

Sometimes teens with an authoritarian parent become very discouraged. These teens believe the parent is "right," so the teen must be "wrong." They don't want to be criticized. So they may try to please the parent. They do exactly what the parent wants. On the surface, this kind of family life may look ideal. After all, the

Three Styles of Parenting

- **Giving orders. With this style, parents sets lots of limits. They try to control their teenagers. They give teens little or no freedom.**
- **Giving in. With this style, parents give teenagers lots of freedom, but few or inconsistent limits.**
- **Giving choices. With this style, parents balance freedom and limits. They give—and expect—respect.**

teenager is well behaved! The parent seems to have won the power struggle. But the price of winning is too high. Teenagers lose their self-respect and don't learn to think for themselves.

- **The authoritarian method doesn't help build trust or respect.**
- **It doesn't offer freedom or responsibility.**
- **It doesn't teach teenagers to think for themselves.**

Giving In

Some parents think it's natural for teens to rebel. They accept that teenagers are hard to live with. These parents think the best approach is to stay out of a teen's way. They give in, letting their teens do whatever they want.

Giving in is also called *permissive* parenting. Permissive parents avoid conflict at all costs. They feel powerless to deal with problems like drug abuse, teen sex, vandalism, and disrespect for authority. They decide that they have no way to keep these things from happening with their teenager.

Some parents feel guilty. They may work a lot and seldom see their teenagers. They may be divorced, or in a new marriage. They may believe they have to make things up to their children. So they don't want to deal with problems.

Giving in like this takes away respect from *both* parents and teens. Teens seem unable to control themselves, cooperate, or change. Parents seem helpless, unable to do their job as a parent.

What Do Teens Learn?

Teens often see giving in as a sign of weakness. Then they seem to have an excuse for rebelling or showing disrespect. They can be quick to grab this power.

For a while, teens may feel good about being allowed to do whatever they want. But not for very long.

Nadia tells her school counselor that she knows her father doesn't care about her. She says, "I come home two hours past curfew all the time. He never says anything. If he loves me, why doesn't he say something to show he cares?" Nadia's father may love his daughter very much. But by being permissive, he sends a different message.

When a parent gives in, teens sense that the parent doesn't respect them. Then they find it hard to respect themselves.

Permissive parents give teenagers a license to misbehave.

- Having no limits at all won't help teenagers learn to get along with others.
- It won't help them learn responsibility.
- won't help them feel good about themselves.

Giving Choices

What approach to parenting *will* help us guide teenagers to be responsible? Consider a *democratic* style. A democratic style balances *rights* and *responsibilities*. It aims to help teenagers become responsible by:

- showing respect
- giving them opportunities to make decisions

The democratic style gives teens their say, but not always their way.

Respect Is Important

Our job as a parent is to provide guidance and discipline for our teenagers. But we also have a responsibility to treat our teens with *respect*.

Parents often complain that their teens do not respect them. Yet many times, adults show teens a lack of respect. How? They nag, yell, hit, or talk down. They may do things for teens that teens can do for themselves. Being too permissive or following a double standard is also disrespectful.

Having a double standard doesn't teach teens respect.

We Had Parents Too

Our parents' style affects our approach to parenting. We accept or reject it as our own style.

- We may have been brought up to believe we must be the best at everything we do. So we may push our teenagers. We may want others to think our teens are the smartest, or the most talented, or the strongest.

- We may have been brought up to believe that we deserve to have our own way. So we may try to force our teenagers to do exactly what we want. Or we may expect other people to do as our teens wish.

- We may have been brought up to respect others. Then we will probably expect other people to do the same. We'll teach our teens to show respect to us, to themselves, and to other people.

In a democratic family, no one is considered more or less important than anyone else. You show respect when you treat your teenager like an equal.

- Does this mean that you are both the same? No. You have more life experiences than your teenager. You have more responsibilities. But both you and your teen are human beings. You both deserve respect.

- Does it mean that your teenager can tell you what to do? Does it mean that your teen doesn't need discipline? No. Your job is to guide your teenager respectfully.

Raina, 13, has been on the phone for twenty minutes. Her mom wants to make a call. Mom gives a signal. Raina says to her, "Okay— in just a minute." Ten minutes later, Raina is still on the phone. Mom's call isn't an emergency. She decides not to interrupt her daughter.

At last, Raina hangs up the phone. Mom says, "I thought you knew that I needed to make a call." Raina says, "I couldn't hang up. Kirsten has a problem. She needed to talk to me."

Mom says, "I understand that you need to talk to Kirsten. But a half-hour is a long time. I have to be able to use the phone when I need it too." Raina says, "Sometimes <u>you</u> stay on the phone when <u>I'm</u> waiting to use it." Mom says, "I've got to make my call now. Let's sit down this weekend and talk. We'll see if we can figure out some phone rules that will work for both of us."

If you want respect, give respect.

Mom could have interrupted Raina's call. She could have forced Raina to get off the phone. She could have gotten angry. She could have said to Raina, "*I* pay for the phone, and so *I* set the rules for using it!" She could have said that Raina's phone calls aren't as important as hers. But would Raina feel respected? Would she respect her mom? Would she want to cooperate? By treating Raina with respect, Mom opens the door for her to be respectful too. She sets the stage for Raina to cooperate and be responsible.

Does this mean that Mom is giving in? No. Mom lets Raina know that phone use needs to be fair for both of them. She sets up a way for them to solve this problem together.

Teens Need to Learn to Make Decisions

Teenagers are becoming adults. They must learn to make decisions. They need practice making choices and living with the results of their choices. Our giving orders doesn't help teenagers learn to do this. Neither does giving in.

Enrico is 16. He wants a car, so he gets a part-time job. His job will pay for insurance and gas, but not expensive repairs. Enrico's parents are glad he is willing to work for something he wants. But they worry that Enrico won't be able to afford repairs on a "junker." They wish he'd save a bit more for a better car. So they give their son a choice.

He may buy the junker. If he does, Enrico must pay for all repairs. If the car breaks down, he'll share the family car with his parents or find other rides.

Enrico decides to buy the junker. Before long, things go wrong with it. The repairs are expensive, and soon Enrico can't even drive it. He has to get rides with friends and use the family car. His parents respect his decision. They don't say, "We told you so." And they don't give Enrico money to help pay his car expenses.

Enrico's decision has given him a good learning experience. By letting him make his own decision, Enrico's parents have helped him. What if they had refused to let him buy the junker? Enrico might have been angry. He would not have learned to make good choices. What if they had rescued him by paying for repairs? He would not have learned to live with his choice.

What Do Teens Learn?

As parents stop trying to control their teenagers, teens begin to change. But change doesn't happen overnight, and things may get worse before they get better. As parents who once gave in begin to show an interest, teens feel more respected and loved. Slowly, teenagers will be able to trust their parents more. These changes won't come overnight. But with time, teenagers are likely to begin to act more responsibly.

The Teen Years Are a Time of Change

Do you remember being a teenager? You were no longer a child. Yet you weren't an adult. It was a time of change and confusion. Today's teenagers are in the same position. In fact, for them, being a teenager is probably *more* confusing, exciting, dangerous, and fun. Magazines, TV, radio, movies, computers, books, tapes, CDs, videos—all give teens messages about the world and their place in it. So do other teenagers, teachers, parents, and people in the community.

Thinking About Parenting Styles

Think about your own teenage years.

- What parenting style did they use?

- How did you feel? What did you do?

Now think about your relationship with your teen.

- What parenting style are you using? What message is this sending to your teen?

- How could you start to change?

For Teens:
Confusion, Problems, and Possibilities

Most teens can't help but be aware of the possibilities and problems in the world—and in their own lives. At times, they can't wait to join the world of adults. At other times, they'd rather never grow up. They want to have a good time, yet want to be taken seriously. They may be bored and look for excitement. They may be busy and worried about how to get everything done. They worry about how they look and what to wear. They worry about the future.

Teenagers' bodies are changing. This affects them physically, emotionally, and mentally. Most teenagers become self-conscious about their changing bodies. They feel that no one is like them, yet they want to be like their friends. They may be moody. They may "try on" different ways of acting and dressing. They may take risks.

- **Dana used to beg to go out for hamburgers. Now she has decided to be a vegetarian.**
- **Wang used to be quiet and polite. Now he swears a lot.**
- **Rosa has found a new group of friends who like to hang out at the mall.**
- **Tom waited years to go out for varsity football. Now he decides not to try out.**
- **Arnetta once worked to keep younger kids off drugs. Now her dad has found marijuana in her coat pocket.**

For Parents: A New Role

Changing from parenting a child to parenting a young adult is difficult. You might feel sad to see your son or daughter leaving childhood. You might worry about sex, drugs, violence, eating habits, grades, or friends. You're not alone. Many parents also have trouble accepting their teenager's growing independence. Feeling unneeded is hard.

But as they mature, teenagers become more independent. They want to be more able to make decisions for themselves. They want to take charge of their lives. It's a healthy sign when teens want to decide who their friends will be and how they'll spend their time.

Independence and responsibility go hand in hand. Giving one without the other is asking for trouble. Sometimes, teenagers grab the independence and push away the responsibility.

Qenla is 16. She's eager to use the car. But she doesn't fill the gas tank. One night her dad says, "I was late to work today because there was no gas in the car." Qenla says, "I didn't use much gas." Dad says, "You can use the car as long as you watch the gas gauge. If it goes below a quarter of a tank, you need to put in gas."

Ben is 13. He wants to be left alone to do his homework. But he has trouble sticking to the job. He starts to look up something on the Internet. Soon he's playing computer games. Today he got a D on his test. He tells his mom, "It's not fair. I studied all night for this test!" His mom doesn't say, "If you'd paid attention to what you were doing, you would have done better." Instead, she calmly asks Ben, "Why do you think you didn't do as well as you wanted?" She helps Ben think about how he studied. She opens the door to talking about it. Maybe she can help him think about a better way to study.

As teens increase the responsibility they take for themselves, parents don't need to control them or be responsible for them as much. This is a tricky balancing act that goes on throughout the teen years. If you and your teen work to develop trust, you can allow your teen to begin to make more decisions. You will be able to listen to your teen's feelings and beliefs. You can guide your teen by telling your own opinions and values. Your teen can make decisions within limits. Each decision will have a *consequence*—a result that happens because of that decision. Help your teenager learn to accept those consequences and learn from them.

Anli, who is 14, has been saving money from her allowance all fall. She wants to buy holiday presents for her friends. Getting ready to go shopping, she puts all her money in her wallet. She puts the wallet in her backpack.

At the mall, Anli stops for something to eat. She leaves her backpack on the floor while she goes to the rest room. When she returns, her wallet is gone. Anli calls her dad on the phone, crying. He says he'll come help her report the theft.

Afterward, Anli says, "I hardly bought any of my presents. Can you help me pay for the others?" Dad says, "You worked hard to save the money, Anli. I know how disappointed you are." Anli cries, "But what am I going to do? Don't you even care that I lost all my savings?" Dad says, "I'll be glad to help you figure out ways to get presents." Anli asks unhappily, "What am I supposed to do without any money?" Her dad says, "I don't know. Would you like to talk about it? Maybe the two of us could come up with some ideas." Anli says rudely, "Like that stupid 'gift certificate' you gave me to help out with chores? My friends won't want presents like that!"

Anli's dad stays respectful. He says, "I'm willing to help, but not if I'm treated rudely. Let me know when you're ready to be respectful, and we'll talk about what to do."

Like Anli's dad, you may find that your teen takes the independence but not the responsibility. In *Parenting Teenagers* you will learn many ways to provide guidance and discipline. This helps teenagers to become independent and responsible. You will also learn discipline that helps teens learn to make better decisions.

Why Are Friends So Important?

For teenagers, being accepted by *peers*—friends and others of the same age—is everything. To many teens, it is more important than being accepted by parents. Often it is more important than *anything* else. Dressing like their friends, listening to the same music, going to the same movies, and being invited to the same parties are important to teenagers.

Some parents wonder, "Why can't teenagers think for themselves? Why do they want to be like all the other kids?" Teenagers must find ways to *belong* outside of the family. This is a necessary step in becoming an adult.

Do you remember when your teenager was a toddler? Did you hear "Mine!" a lot? Before learning to share, your 2 year old had to understand the meaning of *ownership*. This was a stage in your child's development. Becoming independent is a stage of a teen's development. Your teen begins to belong outside the home. With time, your teen will start to feel more independent and capable. Then your teen begins to be more willing to think and act alone.

Teenagers seek to belong with peers in many ways. Sometimes they do it by studying and learning skills. They may take part in plays, sports, or music activities. They may join clubs, become volunteers, or get jobs. There are other ways to belong too. Teens may want to dye their hair, pierce their nose, or get a tattoo. They may want to dress in certain ways. They may smoke, drink, use other drugs, or have sex. They may drive fast or take risks. They may get involved in shoplifting, vandalism, or other illegal activities. They may join a gang. Often teens use both positive and negative ways to belong.

Teenagers must find ways to belong outside the family. This is a step to becoming an adult.

Teens *experiment* as they search for ways to belong. They "try on" behaviors. How we react to a behavior can encourage teens to keep acting that way or to choose a different behavior. Later in this chapter, we'll look more closely at that idea.

Who Owns the Problem?

Teens are learning to make decisions that are different from the ones their parents would make for them. Most of us did this ourselves. Many of the decisions teenagers make are not dangerous or irresponsible. When this is the case, your best response is to listen, watch, and try to understand. Many of the issues that tend to cause conflict between parents and teens don't need to.

How do you decide when to get involved and when not to? For now, start by asking yourself, "Who does this problem belong to? Me? Or my teenager?" In other words, who "owns" the problem?

To decide who owns a problem, ask yourself these four questions:

1. **Are my rights being disrespected?**
2. **Could anybody get hurt?**
3. **Is someone's property threatened?**
4. **Is my teen unable to take this responsibility?**

- If the answer to *any* of these questions is "yes," then you own the problem—or you and your teen own it together.
- If the answer to *every* question is "no," then your teenager owns the problem.

Often, the teenager owns the problem. Issues like how allowance is spent, hairstyle, clothing, and music are often best left up to teens. By making decisions involving those issues, they are learning about their own goals and values.

Sometimes the parent owns the problem. You may be bothered because your teen swears or leaves a mess all over your home. You're the one who owns this problem.

With teens, many problems are shared. A teen may be depressed or failing in school. The teen may use drugs, be involved in a gang, or be in trouble with the police. Both the parent and the teen own problems like these.

The person who owns the problem is responsible for solving it. Knowing this, you can decide *not* to get involved in problems that belong only to your teen. This can help you avoid conflicts with your teen. We'll talk more about owning and solving problems in Chapter 4.

Thinking About Your Changing Teenager

Remember when you were a teenager.

- **What was it like to be neither a child nor an adult?**
- **What did you do to belong <u>outside</u> of your home?**

Now think about your own teenager.

- **What changes are happening for your teen?**
- **What are some things that are causing conflict between you?**
- **Which of these are things you might be able to "let go" of? Which aren't?**

Work to let go of some things. Think about some ways to approach the other things. How can you be respectful? How can you help your teen make a better decision?

Why Do Teenagers Misbehave?

Teenagers have a basic goal: to feel that they belong. To do this, they may use positive behavior or misbehavior.

Rudolf Dreikurs, a well-known psychiatrist, discovered that when children misbehave, they are *discouraged*. This applies to teenagers as well as to younger children. They want to belong, but they do not believe they can belong in useful ways. They find that misbehavior pays off. It helps them feel that they belong.

Children and teenagers try to belong in four common ways. Each way is a kind of misbehavior. Dreikurs called these the *four goals of misbehavior*. Understanding these goals can help you know what teens want when they misbehave. This can help you decide how to guide them to more positive behavior.

The Goals of Teen Misbehavior

The goals of misbehavior are:

- **attention**
- **power**
- **revenge**
- **displaying inadequacy**

Identifying the Goal

Before you can guide your teen, you need to know what goal the teen is after. To identify the goal, look at three clues:

- **how you *feel* when the misbehavior happens**
- **what you *do* about the misbehavior**
- **how your teen *responds* to what you do**

In this chapter, we'll look at how you can identify each of the goals of misbehavior. Then, in Chapter 2, we will look more closely at the goals and at what to do when your teen misbehaves.

Attention

Children of all ages need *attention*. This goal appears more in some teenagers than in others. If teenagers can't get attention in useful ways, then they seek it by misbehaving.

A teen who misbehaves for attention will do something that the parent finds annoying. The parent steps in to correct the misbehavior. The teenager has gotten attention. All may be well for a short while. But before long, the teenager repeats the misbehavior or finds another way to get the parent's attention.

Thinking About Problems and Parenting Styles

When parents give orders . . .
Some parents tend to feel that <u>all</u> problems belong to them. This is often true of authoritarian parents—those who give orders. Do you tend to feel this way? If so, deciding who owns the problem could help you avoid power struggles.

When parents give in . . .
Permissive parents tend to avoid and ignore problems, even serious ones. Do you find yourself giving in and giving up much of the time? If so, deciding who owns the problem could help you choose when to get involved.

When parents give choices . . .
If you are a parent who tends to give choices, deciding who owns the problem can help you too. It can help <u>all</u> parents decide when to walk away, when to help, and when to feel responsible. This can help your relationship with your teen.

Teens find many ways to get a parent's attention.

Sometimes teenagers seek attention quietly. A teen might do nothing, expecting to be waited on. This is *passive* attention.

Power

Many teenagers seek the goal of *power*. A teen who does this is telling the parent, "You can't make me!" or "You'd better do what I want!" The teen might yell or fight with the parent. The teen might break the rules. It's a way the teen shows independence.

It's Wednesday night. Jared's mom is at work. His stepdad, Eddie, is at a meeting. Jared knows that friends aren't allowed at home when both Mom and Eddie are gone. Last week friends were over, and Eddie warned Jared not to do that again. But two friends stop over, and Jared lets them in. Eddie comes home and finds the boys there. He is angry. "Jared," he says loudly. "You know the rules about friends when your mom and I aren't home!" Jared yells, "We're just watching TV! We didn't hurt anything!" Eddie frowns. "Well," he says, "it better not happen again. I mean it!"

When a teenager seeks power, the parent feels angry. If the parent fights, the teen fights back. If the parent gives in, the teenager has won the power struggle and so stops misbehaving.

Choice of friends is a common power issue for teens and parents. Parents don't always like the friends. Then they may try to get the teenager to choose different friends.

Sometimes a teen will do what the parent wants, but will do it slowly or sloppily. This is a form of passive power. The teen is saying, without words, "You can make me do this, but I'll do it *my* way. You can't make me do it *your* way."

Revenge

Some teenagers believe they can't win a power struggle with parents. They decide that the way to belong is to get even—to seek *revenge*. Teens with a goal of revenge believe they are not lovable. They think they can find their place in the family or at school only by being cruel and hurting others.

Meg lives with her mother, a single parent. Meg wants to date a boy named Todd. Meg is 15 and Todd is 18. Mom feels Todd is too old for Meg. She tells Meg no. Meg is furious. That night, while Mom is in the shower, the phone rings. It's David—Mom's boyfriend. Meg sees a chance to get revenge. She says to David, "Mom's in the shower. She's getting ready for a date with someone else. I'll tell her you called."

Later on, Meg's mom calls David. He tells her what Meg said to him. Mom is angry and hurt. She hangs up the phone and goes to Meg's room. She says, "I'll teach you to lie about me to David! You're grounded. And I'm taking the phone out of your room. No phone conversations with Todd—period!"

When teens want revenge, they may say or do something hurtful. Or they may stare angrily at the parent. This is passive revenge. The parent feels hurt and may want to get even. But by punishing a teenager who seeks revenge, the parent gives a new reason for the teen to seek more revenge. The result is often a growing "war" of revenge. Both the teen and the parent have angry, hurt feelings.

Sometimes teens go after thrills.

Some teens take risks to get revenge. To seek thrills is natural for teenagers. Sometimes they seek excitement too often. Then the parents feel shocked, hurt, or angry. They feel worried, too, about what the teenager might do next. Seeing their parents' shock or worry, the teens decide to go after more thrills. Often, this may turn into a power struggle too.

Displaying Inadequacy

Teens who *display inadequacy* are the most discouraged of all. These teens have a very low opinion of themselves. They don't believe they can do something, so they give up. They show parents (and themselves) that they just *can't* make friends, gain or lose weight, figure out homework, or do a good job at chores. Their way to belong is to get others to expect nothing of them. When a teen gives up, the parent feels like giving up too. If the parent *does* give up, the teenager's goal has been met. The parent has "agreed" to expect nothing from the young person.

For most teens, giving up is not total. It usually happens in a certain area, such as schoolwork, sports, or another activity. Where teenagers feel unable to succeed, they may stop trying.

Combining Goals

Teenagers may seek more than one goal at a time. Also, how teens behave outside of the family often affects the teen-parent relationship. The behavior can get negative attention from parents. Struggles for power and revenge can occur:

- **A girl may go to lots of drinking parties. She may want revenge or power as well as excitement and peer acceptance.**
- **A boy may like to watch violent movies. He could be after both power and peer acceptance.**
- **A boy may choose friends his mom doesn't like. He may be using peer acceptance to get Mom's attention.**
- **A girl may be a math whiz—while Dad can't balance the checkbook. The teen might use this skill for power or revenge.**
- **A girl may have sex because she wants to be accepted by her boyfriend. She may find it exciting. She might also seek power in an area her parent can't control.**
- **A teen may smoke for excitement and peer acceptance. Smoking can also be a way to seek power when a parent tries to control the teen's activities.**

Swearing and crude language are often a bid for power or revenge.

- A teen may use drugs for excitement. But she could also be using them as an escape. This might be displaying inadequacy—showing that she can't meet the challenges of living.

- A teen may join a gang or another group that sets him apart from others. He may be seeking power as well as peer acceptance.

The point of talking about goals of misbehavior isn't to prove how "bad" teenagers are. The point is to understand the misbehavior and your reaction to it. Only by doing this can you break old patterns and start new ones. As you change the way you respond, you begin to influence your teen in new ways.

The Flip Side: Positive Beliefs

Each of the goals of misbehavior has a "flip side"—a positive belief that can lead to better behavior goals.

- **Involvement:** "I want to be a part of things. Please help me learn to contribute."

- **Independence:** "I want to be independent. Please let me make decisions and learn from them."

- **Fairness:** "I want things to be fair. Please give me a chance to cooperate."

- **Being competent:** "I need time to think by myself. I want to succeed. Please help me learn to trust myself."

Knowing the flip side of the four goals is helpful. We can use this information to help our teens move:

- from attention to involvement
- from power to independence
- from revenge to fairness
- from displaying inadequacy to being competent

How Can I Start to Build a Better Relationship With My Teenager?

You have seen that strong relationships are built on respect. Three other ingredients for strong relationships are:

- having fun
- giving encouragement
- showing love

The key to knowing the teen's goal is to look at how you feel, what you do, and how your teenager responds.

Having Fun

Often, when children reach the teen years, fun family times happen less and less. This is due to many things. The relationship may be difficult. The teen might be more interested in friends. Everyone is busy. Even so, having fun with our teenagers is important. Having fun lets you and your teen get away from focusing on problems.

Fun doesn't need to take lots of time. Where to begin?

- **Start the day with a good-morning smile. This can set the tone for your teen's whole day—and for yours.**

- **Be willing to laugh at yourself. When you see humor in your own problems, teens can see it in theirs. When you laugh at your mistakes, teenagers are reminded that mistakes are okay.**

- **Let fixing meals or shopping for groceries together become times to talk, share stories, or even be a little silly. On the bus or in the car, share a funny experience with your teen. Watch a funny TV show while you fold laundry together.**

- **"Tune in" to your teen's sense of humor. Laugh together over something you hear on the radio. Share a humorous article in a magazine.**

- ***Planning* some enjoyable time together is also a good idea. Aim to do this at least once a week. You might rent a video, jog, go to a movie, or visit a museum. Take advantage of unplanned time together too. If the moment is a good one, savor it!**

Giving Encouragement

We must believe in our teenagers if they are to believe in themselves:

- To feel capable and loved, teenagers need lots of encouragement.

- To be ready to truly cooperate, teenagers need to feel good about themselves.

Every person is unique. Your teenager has many special and wonderful qualities. When you notice these qualities and point them out, your teenager will feel *encouraged*. With each bit of encouragement, young people grow to like themselves better.

Encouragement means giving less importance to mistakes and more importance to your teenager's strengths. It focuses on efforts and tells your teen, "I have confidence in you."

Don't Forget to Laugh!

Humor can ease many tense situations. And it can remind your teenager that you are a fun person!

- Mom says to Audra, "Why, yes, I <u>do</u> use as many dishes as possible when I know it's your turn to clean up. Do you mean to tell me that scrubbing dirty pans <u>isn't</u> your favorite thing to do?"

- Jordan often forgets to walk Kaya, the family dog. On Thursday, Kaya can't wait anymore. She has an accident in the kitchen. Unhappy, Jordan cleans up. On Friday, Jordan remembers Kaya late in the day. He calls, "Come on, Kaya!" Kaya runs to the door. The phone rings. Jordan answers and chats for ten minutes. When he gets back to the door, Kaya is waiting next to a puddle. Grandpa says to Jordan, "At least you're doing better! This time Kaya almost got out the door!"

It's hard to predict when your teen might want your company.

Create
a home
atmosphere
where your
teen feels
encouraged.

Showing Love

Though they are no longer children, teenagers still need to feel a parent's love. Show love by your words and by your actions:

- **by saying "I love you"**
- **by giving hugs and pats on the back**
- **by doing things you know your teen likes—such as fixing a favorite meal**
- **by speaking and acting with respect**
- **by allowing your teen to grow in responsibility and independence**

You Have Taken the First Big Step

In Chapter 1, you have learned many things about yourself and your teen:

- You have seen the importance of respect.
- You have seen that your teenager needs opportunities to make decisions.
- You have thought about the ways your teen is changing.
- You have learned that your teen wants to belong.
- You have looked at ways to show respect, encouragement, and love for your teen.
- You have remembered how important enjoying each other is.

In doing these things, you have taken an important step in meeting your parenting challenge.

THIS WEEK

Notice your teenager's behavior and how you respond to it. Decide what the goal is. Ask yourself:

1. What did my teen do?
2. How did I feel?
3. What did I do about it?
4. What did my teen do then?
5. What do I think the goal of misbehavior was?
6. What is one way I could encourage a more positive goal?

Encouragement STEP

How do you feel about being the parent of a teenager? Think about how you feel right now.

- **If you feel good, why? What are you doing that you feel good about?**
- **How can you keep that good feeling?**

Think of at least <u>one thing</u> about parenting that was encouraging today.

- **Why is it encouraging?**
- **How could you do more of that thing?**

Chapter 3 deals with encouragement. Each chapter of this book has an "Encouragement Step" to help you get in the encouragement habit. Throughout the book, you'll also find short activities that let you focus on yourself— because you need encouragement too!

JUST FOR YOU

Ease the Stress

It's hard work to solve problems with teenagers. You may find yourself feeling stress. *Stress* is a response to upsetting events. It can be something physical: a headache, high blood pressure, a racing heart. It can be emotional: You might feel worried or have trouble sleeping. You might want to scream.

You know these reactions aren't good for you. But what can you do about them? Here are a few ideas:

1. **Use deep breathing.** Breathe deeply for fifteen seconds. Let your breathing pace itself. Say "calm" as you breathe in. Say "down" as you breathe out. "Calm… down…."

2. **Use self-talk.** Say simple, upbeat things to yourself: "Be calm." "Take it easy." "You're okay." "This will pass."

3. **Be prepared.** If you think something is going to be stressful, be ready for it. Take a few deep breaths. Talk to yourself *before* facing the situation.

4. **Take a new look.** Think of a hard situation as a challenge—not as something that you can't handle. See it as a chance to find new strength in yourself.

5. **Pat yourself on the back.** Accept yourself. Take time every day to think about your good qualities. Tell yourself: "I'm capable." "I'm worthwhile." "I make my own decisions."

6. **Keep a journal.** Write about stressful situations. Note what you did to help yourself ease the stress. Write yourself notes about how well you are doing.

For Your *Family*

This activity won't take long. Do it when your family is together—perhaps at mealtime.

- **Take turns telling about something good that happened to each of you during the day.**

- **At first, you might want to start the conversation. Or ask your teen: "What is something nice that happened to you today? Tell us about it."**

Do this family sharing as often as you can.

POINTS TO REMEMBER

1. Your parenting challenge is to raise a teenager who is healthy, confident, cooperative, and responsible.

2. You can't make your teenager change. You can change your own approach and build a better relationship with your teen.

3. Treat your teenager with respect.

4. Encourage responsibility and cooperation by giving your teenager chances to make decisions.

5. Your teenager is changing physically, emotionally, and mentally. This affects your teen's behavior.

6. Knowing who owns the problem can help you decide when to get involved in your teenager's problems. The person who owns the problem is responsible for solving it.

7. To decide who owns a problem, ask yourself:
   - Are my rights being disrespected?
   - Could anybody get hurt?
   - Is someone's property threatened?
   - Is my teen unable to take this responsibility?

   If the answer to *any* question is "yes," you—or you and your teen—own the problem. If the answer to *every* question is "no," your teenager owns the problem.

8. All children, including teenagers, want to belong. They get a feeling of belonging through both useful behavior and misbehavior.

9. The four goals of misbehavior are:
   - attention
   - power
   - revenge
   - displaying inadequacy

10. You can build a good relationship with your teenager by:
    - showing respect
    - having fun
    - giving encouragement
    - showing love

Chart 1

IDENTIFYING THE GOALS OF TEEN MISBEHAVIOR

How do you feel?	What do you usually do?	How does your teen usually respond?	Goal of misbehavior	"Flip Side" of the goals
Annoyed	Remind, nag, coax	Stops temporarily. Later, misbehaves again	Attention	Involvement
Angry, threatened	Punish, fight back, give in	Continues to misbehave, defies you, or does what you've asked slowly or sloppily	Power	Independence
Very hurt, angry	Get back at teen, punish	Misbehaves even more, keeps trying to get even	Revenge	Fairness
Hopeless, like giving up	Give up, agree that teen is helpless	Does not respond or improve	Displaying inadequacy	Being competent

CHAPTER TWO

Changing **Your** *Response to* **Your Teen**

You've learned that your teen needs to belong. Misbehavior is one way teenagers seek to do this. They discover that misbehavior works for them—it gives them a payoff. What's the payoff? In relationships with parents, it's how the parents respond.

What Can I Do When My Teen Misbehaves?

Your teenager chooses to misbehave. The way you respond, however, is up to you. If you respond as expected, your teenager gets the desired payoff. But if you respond in some other way, you can send a completely different message. With your words and actions, you show that you won't give the payoff your teen wants. Over time, this gives your teenager a chance to choose positive goals and positive behavior.

This won't happen overnight. This whole book is about how you can support your teen's positive goals. But you must start someplace. A good place to begin is by breaking the pattern. Decide how your teenager expects you to respond and *do the opposite.*

Let's look at some examples.

Here's what you will learn . . .

- Your teenager has beliefs about how to belong.

- Your teen's feelings and behaviors come from these beliefs.

- You can listen to hear what your teen is thinking and feeling.

- You can show your teen that talking about feelings is okay.

- You can change your relationship by changing <u>your</u> response to your teenager.

A misbehaving teenager is discouraged.

Attention

It's Friday morning. Reba, 13, walks into the kitchen. She stands by the counter and waits for her mom to notice her. Mom looks up from the paper. She sees Reba and feels annoyed. Mom says, "Reba—you can't go to school in that top. I can see your belly button!" Reba says, "This is Kay's shirt, and she wears it all the time. I think it looks nice!" "Go and change," says Mom. Reba sighs, "Oh, all right."

Five minutes later, Reba's back. Mom takes one look at her and rolls her eyes. "You can't wear those ripped-up jeans! For pity's sake, Reba, why won't you put on something decent?" Reba says, "Okay, okay." She hurries off and returns, wearing clean jeans and blouse. Mom says, "That's better."

Reba eats some cereal. She goes back to the bedroom for her books. When she returns to the kitchen, Mom sees that Reba has put on eye shadow. Mom sighs and says, "Now look at you! That's way too much eye shadow!" Mom takes a tissue and wipes off some of the eye makeup.

Clues to Reba's Goal

1. Mom feels *annoyed.*
2. Mom gives attention: She *nags* and *criticizes.*
3. Reba *stops misbehaving for a while.* Later, she *does something else* to get Mom's attention.

Reba's goal is *attention.*

What Else Could Mom Do?

- She could ignore Reba's clothes and makeup. She could simply say "Good morning" and talk about something else.

- She could let the school decide if Reba's shirt or jeans fit the dress code. If they don't, Mom won't need to say anything. It will be up to Reba to find an outfit in her closet that's okay for school.

- Instead of noticing clothes or makeup, Mom can notice something positive. She might say, "It's nice to see you up so early!" Or she might ask, "What's going on for you in school today?"

- At other times, she needs to give positive attention to her daughter.

Power

Peter is 16. Lately he's been spending a lot of time with Mark, a new friend. Mark doesn't like to come to Peter's home. Instead, he wants Peter to go places with him at night. Peter doesn't talk to his dad as much as he used to. He isn't home most nights. Dad is worried. He doesn't always know where Peter is.

One night as Peter heads out the door, Dad asks, "Where are you going?" Peter says, "Out! Do you need to know every place I go?" Dad feels angry. He says, "Don't talk to me that way! I have a right to know where you go—and who you're with!"

"Gimme a break!" Peter says loudly. "Me and Mark are just gonna hang out. It's no big deal." Dad says, "I don't like this 'hanging out' with Mark. You stay home tonight and do homework. Your grades could use it!"

Peter says, "My grades are fine!" Dad says angrily, "They won't be if you keep running around with guys like Mark instead of studying!"

Peter glares and asks, "What's wrong with Mark?" Dad says, "He's not like your other friends. I don't trust him." Peter shouts, "That's so stupid! You don't even know him. If you think you can pick my friends, you're wrong! I'm outta here!" Peter rushes out the door, slamming it behind him.

Clues to Peter's Goal

1. Dad feels *angry.*
2. Dad *tries to correct* Peter by *laying down the law.*
3. Peter *fights back.* He *continues misbehaving.*

Peter's goal is *power.*

Dad may be right to worry about Peter's friendship with Mark. But a fight for power won't help. Starting or joining a fight will just keep the power struggle going.

What Else Could Dad Do?

- Dad could wait until later to talk about this again with Peter— when they're both calm. Then Dad might say, "I don't want to judge Mark unfairly. Could we talk about this together?"

- When they talk again, Dad could start by speaking respectfully. He might say, "It bothers me that Mark doesn't ever come here. Do you think he doesn't feel welcome?"

- Instead of giving orders and criticizing, Dad might say, "I worry about some changes in you since you've been spending time with Mark."

What Is Misbehavior?

- actions or words that are disrespectful or ignore others' rights or safety

- refusal to cooperate

- behavior that is dangerous to the teen

- illegal behavior

- Dad can't really stop Peter from *ever* spending *any* time with Mark. But he has a right to know where his son is. And he has a right to expect Peter to stick to agreed-upon limits or negotiate new ones. (In Chapter 4, you'll look at a way parents and teens can work together in this way.)

- When he has to say no, Dad can do it matter-of-factly, without criticizing or blaming: "You can't go out if I don't know where you are."

Dad knows that choosing new friends is a way for Peter to become independent. Dad is wise not to let friends become a power struggle. By staying calm, he'll leave the door open for Peter to look more carefully at friendships. He'll let Peter save face. Then a new friendship may not become a real problem.

If Dad decides right away that he doesn't like how Mark dresses or acts, Mark will sense these bad feelings. If Mark feels that Peter's dad doesn't like him, he'll avoid Peter's home. Dad can remember, too, that all teens are growing and changing. He may find that Mark has many positive qualities.

Of course, Peter might still refuse to cooperate. Then Dad will need to set limits and consequences. Chapter 5 teaches a method for doing this with your teenager.

Revenge

André is 14. He and his mom have been fighting over lots of big and little things lately.

His mom has built a fence on the patio. She worked hard on it. Now she wants André to paint it. André doesn't want to. "We didn't need a stupid fence!" he says. Mom is very angry and says, "You paint that fence, or no dance for you tonight!"

That night, André comes through the house, all ready to go to the dance. His mom blocks the door and says, "You're not going to the dance tonight. I'll be right here to make sure you don't!" André swears at his mom and shouts, "I hate you!" He runs off, slamming the door as he reaches his room.

Later, Mom goes to bed. When she gets up in the morning, she sees that André splashed paint all over the patio but not a single drop on the fence. She feels hurt and angry.

Clues to André's Goal

1. Mom feels *hurt and extremely angry.*
2. Mom *wants to get back* at André by taking away the dance.
3. André *hurts Mom back* by ruining the patio.

André's goal is *revenge.*

- Mom could refuse to feel hurt and not say anything else that is hurtful.

- She could refuse to get even with André.

- She could talk to André when they are both calm. She could say, "André, we have a problem. I need your help and cooperation. It seems like you are very angry with me. Help me understand what's going on."

Revenge often results from a failed power struggle. André lost his bid to go to the dance without painting the fence. Changing a cycle of revenge takes time. But André can't have a battle of revenge if Mom won't join in. This will give both Mom and André a chance to cool down and think. Mom also needs to look for ways to build trust and respect.

Displaying Inadequacy

Sasha is 15. Since starting at a new school, she has been having trouble with biology. Her dad says to her, "What's wrong with you, Sasha? You did well in biology in your old school." Sasha says, "This biology is way beyond what I've learned. You can't imagine how hard it is. Please let me stay home today. There's a big test, and I know I'm going to flunk it." Sasha starts to cry.

Dad doesn't know what to do. Like Sasha, he also feels she can't do the work. He says to his daughter, "I guess it'd be okay for you to stay home today. I'll call the school. Maybe they can switch you into an easier class."

Clues to Sasha's Goal

1. **Dad feels *hopeless*. He *wants to give up* on Sasha's succeeding with algebra.**

2. **Dad *gives up*. He tells Sasha that he agrees things might be too hard for her.**

3. **Sasha has Dad's permission to fail. She is *not likely to improve* at algebra.**

Sasha has said, "I can't," and Dad has agreed. Sasha's goal is *displaying inadequacy*.

Often, changing your response means doing the opposite of what your teen expects.

What Else Could Dad Do?

- Dad could refuse to give up on Sasha. He might say, "I know you can handle the schoolwork. You just need to get some help. Let's call the school and get an appointment with the counselor to arrange for some help. Maybe there's a student who could help you out."

- He could be careful not to pity Sasha. If Sasha thinks Dad feels sorry for her, she'll feel sorry for herself too.

- He could encourage Sasha as she works on her schoolwork. He can notice small efforts and progress. He might say, "Aha! You've got that formula figured out!" He might say, "I knew you'd get it if you stuck to it."

Sometimes a teen who says "I can't" wants to have attention or power, not to display inadequacy. How can you tell the difference? The teen who displays inadequacy gives up. This young person wants to be left alone or excused from the task. Use your feelings as a guide. Do you feel annoyed or angry? If so, you can guess the teen's goal is attention or power. Do you feel hopeless, like giving up? If you do, the goal is probably to display inadequacy.

A teen who gives up is *very discouraged*. Using lots of support and encouragement with such a teen is important. In Chapter 3 you will learn more about how to encourage your teenager.

Displaying inadequacy is different from serious depression. For a discussion of depression and suicide, see pages 117–19.

We often reinforce teen misbehavior by reacting the way teens expect us to. Avoid this trap by deciding not to act on your first reaction. *Stop, step back,* and *think* before you act by asking yourself: "How do I best respond?" Hard as it is, know that you have to change not only your behavior when your teen misbehaves, but also your feelings. Refuse to be annoyed, angry, hurt, or discouraged. These emotions will only reinforce the misbehavior. The "Just for You" activity on page 45 will help you learn how to change your emotions.

Why Do Teenagers Become Discouraged?

You have seen that teens who misbehave are discouraged. Why do they become discouraged? Beneath teenagers' wish to belong are *beliefs* about how they need to do this. We call beliefs that lead to misbehavior "faulty beliefs."

Faulty Beliefs of Teenagers

- **Attention:** "I belong only by being noticed—even if that makes problems for Dad or Mom."

- **Power:** "I belong only by being the boss—even if that leads to a fight. If I can get Mom or Dad to fight with me, I have power."

- **Revenge:** "I am not lovable. I belong only by hurting others. I want Dad or Mom to feel as hurt as I do."

- **Displaying inadequacy:** "I belong by convincing Mom or Dad that I can't do things. In fact, when I *try* to do something and fail, I *don't* belong. It's better not to try at all."

In Chapter 1, you saw that each of these faulty beliefs has a flip side—a positive belief that can lead to better behavior goals. (See page 16.) We want to encourage our teenagers to seek positive goals. We want to help them develop *all* of the positive beliefs. We want to help them move:

- **from attention to involvement**
- **from power to independence**
- **from revenge to fairness**
- **from displaying inadequacy to being thoughtful and competent**

Every misbehavior has a "flip side."

Where Do Beliefs Come From?

We formed our basic beliefs when we were very young. These came from how we viewed our early family experiences. Our beliefs were not always logical, but they made sense to us. The belief "I'll belong by being good" would create many positive behaviors. But if our chosen behavior doesn't get the result we want, our beliefs can cause us problems. Many of these beliefs remain with us today. We are not even aware of some of them. Sometimes they can cause us problems.

Teenagers have formed beliefs too. Like ours, theirs come from how they see experiences they had when they were very young. We have seen that beliefs can come from the style of parenting. They also come from a teen's view of three other things:

- what's important in the family
- the teenager's place in the family
- what parents say and do

What's Important in the Family

Every family has a unique mood or tone. We call this the *family atmosphere*. Also, adults in every family have *values*. The combination of atmosphere and values gives our children a message about what is important in a family.

Children pay close attention to the atmosphere. Children usually know, for example, if education, religion, sports, or the arts are important to a parent. This is because the parent will enjoy these activities in front of the child and will often teach them to the child.

Some values may not be stated but are still obvious to the teen:

- **When parents talk about problems together, the teen sees the value in cooperation.**
- **When parents argue often and loudly, the teen sees the value in fighting.**
- **When parents refuse to compromise, the teen sees the value in getting one's own way.**

For teens with two parents, a family value is something that's important to both parents. It's a value even if the parents don't agree about it.

Some families include a grandparent or another adult who helps in parenting. This adult's values may then become part of the family atmosphere. Sometimes, the adults in a family don't agree on something or don't share the same value.

Kado and Nori are 17-year-old twins. They live with their mom and grandpa. Grandpa drinks beer and whiskey. Mom's religion doesn't allow drinking. She doesn't drink at all, and she doesn't want her kids to drink either. She asks Grandpa not to drink at home. She argues about it with him. Grandpa makes fun of Mom's religion. He tells Kado and Nori that its rules are stupid. Nori thinks Grandpa is right. Kado doesn't. He wishes Grandpa wouldn't say bad things about religion.

The adults in this family don't agree about what Mom's religion teaches. But it is clear that religion and alcohol are important in Kado and Nori's family. Kado and Nori are both making choices about these issues.

Changes in the family affect the family atmosphere:

- **A single parent marries. The new husband or wife brings family values. The family atmosphere changes.**

- **Parents get separated or divorced. Children often feel the family values more strongly—especially those that parents don't agree on.**

- **A single parent forms a new relationship or remarries. Children may become part of two families with two different family atmospheres.**

It is not helpful to criticize or try to change values that are clearly important to a teenager. Each teenager needs to be accepted as a person. This can be a challenge to many parents.

Vita is newly remarried. Her new husband is Luís. Luís has a son named Hector. Both Hector and Vita's son Julio are 16. When Hector is at his mom's home, he has no curfew. His mom thinks this is okay. Hector expects to have no curfew at his dad's home too. Now Julio thinks he shouldn't have a curfew either.

This is a problem for Vita and Luís. But they don't say anything unkind to Hector. And they don't tell Julio that Hector or his mom is "wrong." Instead, they tell the boys, "Here the curfew is midnight. That's our household rule."

What if the boys refuse to cooperate? Many things might happen. Hector's mom may have to be called and all the adults discuss the situation. Vita and Luís need to stick together on this. They don't want to say hurtful things about Hector's mom to Hector or Julio. They must work to find ways so that Hector will want to cooperate and take part in the family.

Every teen accepts or rejects important family values.

In Chapter 4 you will learn ways to encourage your teen to cooperate. The "For Your Family" activities at the end of each chapter can help you too. For now, understanding how your values affect those of your teen is important.

The Teenager's Place in the Family

Another important influence on beliefs is birth order. It affects the teen's "place" in the family and how teens see themselves. It affects what they believe is important. It affects how they think and act. A teenager may be an only child, the oldest, the second, the middle, or the youngest—the "baby," even as a teen.

An Only Child

Only children grow up being the center of attention. How does this affect them? Sometimes they have trouble getting along with others. Many only children spend a lot of time alone, or with their parents and their parents' friends. They sometimes grow up—or seem to grow up—quickly. They can be highly creative.

An Oldest Child

An oldest child was once an only child. Giving up all the attention can be hard for an oldest child. Often, an oldest child wants to be the boss. Many oldest children also learn to be leaders and to cooperate. They often learn responsibility because the younger children may look to them for help.

A Second Child

A second child never has the parent's full attention the way a first child once did. This child may work hard to keep up with or overtake the older sister or brother. Sometimes a second child decides to be the opposite of the older child. If the older child is usually "good," the second may decide to be "bad."

A Middle Child

A middle child often feels "squeezed" between the older and younger children. Some middle children are not as sure of themselves as only and older children. Many like things to be fair. Often middle children learn ways to get along with all kinds of people. Sometimes, though, they become "problem children" who misbehave to get attention.

Thinking About Your Values

When you were a teenager, were these important to the adults in your family: religion, education, work, money, other values?

- What values did you accept?

- What values did you reject?

What values do you think you're passing on to your teen? What values would you like to pass on?

A Youngest Child

Youngest children usually don't have to do as much for themselves as older ones. These children can be bossy and demanding. Or they can be charming and friendly. Sometimes they use their charm to get help from other people. Some youngest children give up because they can't yet do what older children can do. Others work hard to be more skillful than their brothers and sisters.

What Does the Teen See?

It might seem that a teenager's place is based on birth order. Actually, it is a little more complicated than that. It is based on how a teen *sees* his or her place.

Danielle, 17, and 15-year-old Damita are sisters. Danielle was sick as a child. She got lots of attention. She needed lots of help. Damita was healthy and strong. She took the role of oldest, while Danielle became "the baby." This pattern continued as the girls grew older. Damita became responsible. Danielle became helpless. She gives up easily and wants lots of pampering.

The Place Changes

Each child's place changes as new children come into a family. It also changes when new families begin through divorce or marriage. When the family changes, a teen's view of how to be important often changes too.

A stepfamily might have two children from each parent. There might be two oldest children. These two might compete for the role of "oldest" in the new family.

Children sometimes compete for their place in the family. For example, a firstborn may struggle to keep the place of an "only" child. This competition also affects beliefs and behavior. When children compete, one child succeeds. Another becomes discouraged or fails.

If children are more than five or six years apart, there can be two "sets" of places.

A family might have four kids ages 17, 15, 10, and 8. Both the 17 year old and the 10 year old may feel like oldest children. The 15 year old and the 8 year old might both feel like the youngest.

Looking at Your Place

- Think about when you were a child. What was your actual, birth-order place? Were you first? second? youngest?

- Now think about how you felt. Did you feel like the leader? the boss? the baby? the one in the middle?

- What does this tell you about yourself today?

STRENGTHS OF EACH PLACE IN THE FAMILY

Place	Belief	Strengths
Only	"I need to be the center of attention."	Independent, creative
Oldest	"I need to be the boss."	Responsible, cooperative
Second	"I need to compete."	Hardworking
Middle	"I'm caught in between."	Fair
Youngest	"I need to rely on others."	Charming, able to get own way

What Parents Say and Do

Children learn from what their parents say and do. This remains true even when children are in the teen years. Your actions and words show your teen what is important to you.

Talk About Values

Teenagers are trying on new ideas and values outside and inside the family. When a value is important to you, share it clearly with your daughter or son. Remember to speak respectfully when you do this. You might say:

- "We need to be honest with each other. Otherwise, you won't be able to trust me, and I won't be able to trust you."

- "I'd like us to be respectful in our home. Swearing isn't a respectful way to talk."

Act as You'd Like Your Teen to Act

Your teenager will learn more from what you do than from what you say. Teens watch your behavior, your attitude, and what seems to work for you. Then they choose for themselves the qualities they value and want.

Share important values and ideas clearly with your teen.

Your teen won't agree with all your values. Expect your teen to try on different ways of acting too. At times, you'll be disappointed when your teen seems to be choosing negative values. When you see this happening, think carefully about what your teen might be seeing in your actions:

Jen is 15. She has a new job. All she talks about is how much money she's making and what she wants to buy. She wants to buy clothes and CDs. She wants to look at catalogs and shop with friends. Marin, Jen's stepmom, is worried about Jen's focus on money. One night, Marin realizes that all through dinner the family has talked about money. They've talked about how to raise money to repair the car, paint the kitchen, and take a trip. Marin decides to focus on different subjects for a while.

For parents to do as they say is important:

- If we ask our teenagers not to lie, we must tell the truth to them—and to others too.

- If we ask our teens to be polite, we must treat them and others courteously.

Where Do Feelings Come From?

Through their *beliefs,* teenagers make choices about how to belong. *Feelings,* too, affect how teens decide to belong. At times, teenagers seem to have more than their share of feelings. Growth and change can lead teenagers to be emotional. Where do feelings come from? Why do we feel happy, angry, or sad?

Feelings Come From Beliefs

We often think of feelings as magical things we can't control. We say: "He made me so angry!" Or, "She's going to drive me crazy!" But think about this: Each of us is responsible for the way we feel. Based on our beliefs, we choose how we feel.

Les's basketball team loses a game. Les believes winning is everything. He feels like losing the game is the end of the world. Kavon believes making an effort is what's important. He feels good about how well the team did against a stronger team.

Cara and Laurie both studied hard for a test and got B's. Cara believes she must be the best. She feels sick about her B. Laurie believes a B shows that she's doing well. She is pleased with her grade.

Doing and Saying

Think about a value you want to pass on to your teen.

- **What can you <u>do</u> to show your child that the value is truly important?**

- **What can you <u>say</u> to explain that value?**

Feelings Have a Purpose

Some teenagers believe they can belong by cooperating. Then they create good feelings toward others. The good feelings help them reach their goal of belonging.

When teens believe they must misbehave to belong, they create negative feelings.

A teen throws a temper tantrum so her dad will give in to her.

A teen pouts when his mom says no. His mom gives in because she dislikes the "silent treatment."

Of course, some negative feelings are not misbehavior:

A teen breaks up with a boyfriend or girlfriend. The teen might feel hurt and cry.

A teen works hard on a project. A friend spills soda on it. The teen might feel angry or frustrated.

How can you decide if your teen is using feelings as a way to misbehave? Look at:

- **how you feel**
- **what you do**
- **how your teen responds to what you do**

This will help you decide what to do. If your teen is misbehaving, don't "buy into" the feelings.

Does this mean you always ignore the feelings? No. Keep in mind that you want to change your response and stay respectful. At times, this means ignoring the misbehavior. But often you can do something helpful. *Listen* to what your teen is saying and feeling. Also, you can always respond later, not only at the moment of misbehavior.

Feelings Communicate

Communication is the key to most relationships. Showing feelings is a way of *communicating*.

When our friends have problems or make mistakes, they *communicate* those feelings to us. They may talk. They may cry. We listen and try to help. We think about their feelings. We do this because we respect and value our friends.

We want to treat our teenagers the same way. In doing so, we build a closer relationship.

Treat your teenager like you'd treat your best friend.

We can't always "fix" our teen's problems. We can't make our child's feelings go away. What can we do? We can show that we care and accept the feelings. We show acceptance by our tone of voice and by the words we use. We communicate respect. Listening is better than giving advice. With advice, the teen relies on us—or tunes us out. When we really listen, we give the teen room to think. Research even shows that teens who feel that their parents listen to them and are emotionally close have fewer problems as they grow to be adults.

How Can I Be a Good Listener?

When you are upset, you might talk to a friend about it. You want your friend to listen, understand, and accept what you are feeling. Your teenager wants the same thing.

Listen for Feelings

Why is listening for feelings important? It helps teenagers feel understood. It helps them think about what they are feeling and why. It can help them think through a problem. It lets them know that talking about feelings is okay.

How to Listen for Feelings

Listening for feelings is a skill. It is called *reflective listening*. Reflective listening is helpful when your teen owns a problem. Here is how you do it:

1. **Listen.** Let your body show that you are listening. Stop your other tasks. Look directly at your teenager.

2. **Hear the feeling.** Listen to your teen's words. Ask yourself, "What is my teenager feeling?" Think of a word that describes the feeling. Also ask yourself, "Why is my teen feeling this way? What led to the feeling?"

3. **Use reflective listening.** Reflective listening is repeating *in your own words* what you think your teen feels and says. Think of yourself as a kind of mirror that *reflects* your teen's feelings. You also reflect the *reason behind* the feeling.

With reflective listening, use the words "You feel" and "because":

- "*You feel* hurt *because* Sara's going out with Rico."
- "*You feel* disappointed *because* you didn't get to play in the game."
- "*You feel* impatient *because* you want to go meet your friends."

After a while, this kind of listening will become more natural. Then you can use your own words:

- "Are you jealous because Terry got the scholarship?"
- "You're bored to be with the family tonight."
- "You're pretty excited about the new job!"

Describe feelings as exactly as you can. These are more than "sad, mad," or "glad." Words like "a little, really," or "very" will help you here:

- "You seem a little worried about how you did on the test."
- "You're very angry that I said you couldn't go to a hotel after the dance."
- "It seems like no one cares, and you're feeling really left out."

Look for Feelings Too

Like the rest of us, teenagers don't always use words to communicate. Sometimes they are silent. They may smile, or scowl, or cry. Sometimes they pull away or hang their head. Just listening will not help you find the meaning of these unspoken feelings. You need to *look* at your teen's face and body for feelings too. Then state the feeling you see:

- "The look in your eyes seems to say that you don't believe me."
- "When your face lights up like that, you look very happy."
- "It looks like you're really down. Want to talk about it?"

Teens don't always use words to tell us how they feel.

I wish I knew how he feels ... if only I had a clue.

Words for "Happy" Feelings

appreciated	better	comfortable	excited
grateful	great	happy	pleased
proud	relieved	satisfied	

Words for "Upset" Feelings

angry	bored	confused	disappointed
frustrated	guilty	hurt	left out
put down	miserable	worthless	

Some Things to Keep in Mind

Reflective listening may be new to both you and your teen. Here are some hints to help you as you begin.

Your teenager may be surprised. Your teen will probably notice your new way of listening. He or she might say, "Yeah, that's right," and then walk away. Don't force your teenager to share feelings. You might seem to be snooping. Pushing the teen to talk could lead to a power struggle.

Don't be discouraged if your teen doesn't respond quickly. Instead, wait for another chance to listen and talk about feelings. Your teenager may want to talk. If so, you might ask, "Would you like to tell me more about it?"

Use a respectful tentative, or questioning, tone. You don't know exactly what your teenager is feeling:

Briana comes in at 11:30, a half-hour early. She slams the door, crying. Dad asks, "Did something happen with Dan?"

Briana says, "Dan was fine—until Maureen told him about what happened last summer. She's such a jerk! I could just die!" Dad looks at Briana kindly. He says, "You must have been really embarrassed. Do you want to tell me about it?"

Dad thought Briana must have had a fight with her boyfriend. His guess was wrong. But because of his tentative tone of voice, Briana could tell he cared and wanted to help. He didn't tell her not to cry. He didn't order her not to call Maureen names. Instead, he kept using reflective listening. In these ways, he let Briana know she could talk with him some more if she wanted to.

Check your own feelings. At times, listening for feelings can go too far. It might even become part of a teen's goal of misbehavior. If you think this might be happening, check your own feelings. Are you annoyed? angry? discouraged?

Finding the Feelings

Three feeling words parents often use are "good," "bad," and "upset." These words don't always tell the whole story.

Look at the word lists above. Think about some other feeling words. Think of as many as you can.

Toban got in trouble for spray-painting a building. Now he has to do community service. Toban tells his mom he hates going to work sorting clothes at a shelter. Mom says, "You don't like doing this work." He says that none of the other kids who got in trouble have to do such a hard job. Mom says, "You feel angry because you think it's unfair that you have to do so much work." Toban complains more and more. Mom sees that he wants her to feel sorry for him. She tells her son, "You feel discouraged because it seems like too much work for what you did wrong. I know you'll get through your community service." She doesn't say anything more.

Mom saw that Toban wanted her to be sorry for him. She decided not to be. Still, she stayed respectful. Toban was probably not pleased. But he could see that Mom respected him. And Mom *has* helped her son. She has let him know that his feelings are okay and that he must be willing to take responsibility for his actions.

What to do when you have to say no. Sometimes you have to say no to your teenager. When you do, listen and respond to what your teen is feeling. Then your teen will know you have heard the feelings:

- "I can see that you're angry, but I won't listen to shouting. I'll be in the kitchen if you'd like to talk about it."

- "You're disappointed. You don't think I'm being fair. But I can't send you on an overnight trip without an adult."

If your teenager still tries to argue, leave the room. Later, you can give positive attention. For example, you can play some catch or ask if your teen wants to make a favorite snack with you.

When we respond in this way, our teenagers may not be any happier. But they learn that their feelings are still okay—even when their actions aren't.

Giving feedback isn't always necessary. Your teen's words won't always be about feelings. Then you don't need to respond:

- "Yuck! Look at all those dirty dishes!" A little grumbling doesn't need a response.

- "Can I wait till payday to buy gas?" This might just be a direct request.

Sometimes your teenager won't want to talk. Sometimes you won't be able to talk when your teen wants to. You might say: "You're worried and want to talk about this. Right now, I have to go to work. Can we talk together later? I'll be home at seven."

Don't expect to hear all about it. Sometimes a teenager needs comforting more than talking. Don't pry. Being there without speaking is another way you can help. If your teen wants to cry and get a hug, give the hug. If your teen wants to vent strong feelings, you may not need to say anything at all.

Give it some time. Reflective listening may seem hard at first. Remembering *why* you are doing it is helpful: to show your teenager that you hear, understand, and accept the feelings. Taking time to think before you talk can help you too. You won't say something you don't want to say.

Like any new skill, reflective listening will take time and practice. Keep at it! After a while, it will begin to feel more natural. And you will begin to see how it can help your relationship with your teen.

You Have Taken Another Big Step

In Chapter 2, you have learned more about your teen and yourself. You have learned and started to practice parenting skills too:

- You have begun to think about what to do when your teen misbehaves.

- You have learned about ways teens form their beliefs and feelings.

- You have found that reflective listening shows that you understand. It also helps your teen talk and think about feelings and work through problems.

- You have seen that you can look as well as listen.

Encouragement
STEP

Changing your response is not always easy. It means changing your beliefs, feelings, and ideas so you can respond in a different way. Making this effort is important. Our reactions affect how our teenagers think, act, and learn. Knowing this makes the effort worthwhile.

Here's another way to think about it: Imagine you are walking down the sidewalk. Someone else is walking straight toward you. If you both keep walking straight, you'll bump into each other. So you decide to step aside slightly. You can do the same thing for your teenager and yourself. You can "step aside" and respond in a different way.

When you feel a problem coming, think about how you can respond in a different way.

For Your *Family*

Notice when your teen helps out, cooperates, or takes responsibility. Let your teen know that you notice. Use the words "I appreciate":

- **"I appreciate when you ask before you borrow my clothes. Thank you."**

- **"I appreciated how you helped your cousin when he had a nightmare."**

Encourage everyone in your family to notice and appreciate when others help.

THIS WEEK

Keep paying attention to the goals of misbehavior. When your teen misbehaves, decide what the goal is. Ask yourself:

1. What did my teen do?

2. How did I feel?

3. What did I do about it?

4. What did my teen do then?

5. What do I think the goal of misbehavior was?

6. What are *two or three ways* I could encourage a more positive goal?

Start to notice what you *first* want to say or do when your teenager talks to you, misbehaves, or comes into the room. Stop yourself from talking without thinking. Be aware of your feelings and choose not to feel the way your teen expects. Instead, think of respectful ways to talk with your teen. Use reflective listening as often as you can.

JUST FOR YOU

Changing Your Self-Talk

Many parents get into a habit of a certain kind of "self-talk." They tell themselves, "My teen *must* behave. *I can't stand it* when my teenager misbehaves. It's *awful!*" When we look closely at this self-talk, we easily see why we get upset!

But you can change your self-talk. To do this, look at your own purpose, feelings, and beliefs.

To find your purpose, ask yourself:

- Do I want to give attention, or help my teen be self-reliant?
- Do I want to show who's the boss, or help my teen be independent and responsible?
- Do I want to get even, or show that I understand?
- Do I want to let my teen off the hook, or help my teen be self-confident?

To look at your feelings, ask yourself:

"Am I annoyed? angry? hurt? discouraged? Or am I *determined* to help my child stop misbehaving?"

You do not need to feel angry with your teen. *Talk* to yourself. Talk yourself into feeling calm and capable of changing your response.

To look at your beliefs, ask yourself:

- What am I telling myself?
- What can I tell myself instead?

The more you do this, the better prepared you will be to respond to misbehavior.

POINTS TO REMEMBER

1. To identify a teen's goal, look at:
    *   how you feel when the misbehavior happens
    *   what you do about the misbehavior
    *   how the teen responds to what you do

2. To encourage positive goals, concentrate on changing how you respond. Do or say something your teen does not expect.

3. Beliefs and feelings affect how a teenager decides to belong.

4. Beliefs can come from the style of parenting. They also come from the teen's view of what is important in the family, the teen's place, and what parents say and do.

5. Feelings come from beliefs.

6. Teenagers want parents to hear, understand, and accept their feelings.

7. With reflective listening, you reflect your teen's feeling and the reason for the feeling. You can start by using the words "You feel" and "because":
    *   "*You feel* discouraged *because* the coach isn't putting you in the game."
    *   "*You feel* confused *because* you don't know how you feel about Fiona."

Chart 2

DEALING WITH THE GOALS OF TEEN MISBEHAVIOR

Remember, to decide your teen's goal, look at:

1. how you feel when the misbehavior happens
2. what you do about the misbehavior
3. how your teen responds to what you do

Goal	Examples of misbehavior	What can you do?	Ways to encourage positive goals and beliefs
Attention	*Active:* Clowning, minor mischief, unique dress *Passive:* Forgetting, not doing chores, expecting to be waited on	Don't give attention on demand. Ignore when possible. Don't wait on teen. Give positive attention at other times.	Notice when teen contributes. Show appreciation for positive behavior.
Power	*Active:* Disobeying, demanding, shouting *Passive:* Being stubborn, ignoring parent	Refuse to fight or give in. Withdraw from power contest. If possible, leave room. Let consequence occur for teen.	Let teen make decisions. Express confidence in teen.
Revenge	*Active:* Being rude, saying hurtful things, being violent *Passive:* Staring hurtfully at others	Refuse to feel hurt or angry. Don't hurt teen back. At other times, work to build trust. Help teen feel loved.	Be as fair as you can. Treat teen as equal. Respect others so teen has this model.
Displaying inadequacy	*Passive only:* Quitting easily, not trying, escaping with drugs or alcohol	Do not pity. Stop all criticizing. Notice all efforts, no matter how small. Don't give up on teen.	Focus on teen's strengths, talents. Notice when teen makes wise choices. Encourage teen.

CHAPTER THREE

Communicating Respect and Encouragement

In Chapter 2, you learned the skill of reflective listening. This kind of listening and giving feedback helps you and your teen communicate. In this chapter, we'll look at two other skills that will help you communicate: I-messages and encouragement.

How Can I Talk So My Teen Will Listen?

You have seen how listening and talking go together: You listen for feelings. Then you respond. Let's look at how you can tell your teenager about *your* feelings.

Speak Respectfully

When you talk about a problem with your teen, share your feelings respectfully.

Damon is 13. He and his three friends have been playing football. Now they rush into the kitchen in their wet shoes. They open cupboards with muddy fingers. Dad has just mopped the floor. He wants to yell, "What's the matter with you kids? You're acting like a bunch of animals!"

But Dad thinks before speaking. He says to the boys, "I know you're hungry and tired. But when you bring all this dirt into the kitchen, I feel discouraged because I just cleaned."

Dad felt like yelling. But he knew that would only show Damon and his friends that yelling is a way to solve problems. Instead,

Dad chose to be respectful. He didn't judge the boys by calling them names. He used a special kind of respectful talk to let the boys know how he felt. He used an *I-message*. An I-message simply tells how you feel.

I-Messages Have Three Parts

To use an I-message, do three things:

1. **Tell what is happening.**
2. **Tell what you feel.**
3. **Explain why you feel that way.**

You-Messages Put Teenagers Down

When talking to teenagers (and others), parents often use *you-messages*. You-messages put down, blame, or nag. Often they begin with the word *you:*

- "You stop that!"
- "You should be ashamed."
- "You should know better."

How Do Teens Respond?

When teenagers hear you-messages, they can begin to feel worthless or they may fight back. They might stop listening. You-messages are discouraging. They don't encourage cooperation.

I-Messages Show Respect

A better way to talk about an issue is with an I-message. I-messages tell how you feel when a teen ignores your rights. They focus on you, rather than on your teen. I-messages don't label or blame.

Here is an I-message:

- **"When you don't call, I feel worried because I don't know where you are."**

It uses these words:

1. When   "*When* you don't call,
2. I feel   *I feel* worried
3. because   *because* I don't know where you are."

Here are two more I-messages:

- **"When the milk is left out, I feel annoyed because it spoils."**
- **"When I found the gas tank low, I felt rushed because I had to stop for gas on my way to work."**

Be careful about using the word *you* after *when*. This might be a hidden you-message.

Once you understand the parts of an I-message, use words that feel natural to you:

● **"I feel hurt when I see you smoke—it's so bad for your lungs."**

You can decide if you want to tell about your feeling, or just the problem:

● **"I can't get ready for work until the bathroom's free."**

These are the most important things to remember about I-messages:

● **They focus on you, not your teen.**
● **They do not blame anyone.**

How Do Teens Respond?

I-messages help teenagers understand what their actions mean for you. I-messages also show teens a way to talk about problems without blaming. They see that you think it's important to share feelings and opinions in a way that can help solve a problem.

Think About the Real Problem

At first, explaining your feelings with an I-message might seem hard. Maybe this will help: Most of the time, what teenagers *do* does not bother us. What bothers us is the *result* of what they do.

Chantel doesn't eat right. She skips breakfast. After school, she snacks on chips and cookies she has bought. She's usually not hungry at mealtime. Her parents worry about her health. They are concerned that she'll be tired or get sick. They fear that this will affect her schoolwork.

The Three Parts of an I-Message

I-messages use these words:

1.	When	"<u>When</u> the stove is left on,
2.	I feel	<u>I feel</u> scared
3.	because	<u>because</u> we could have a fire."

Be careful not to let an I-message become a you-message.

Chantel needs to eat a healthy diet. But what really bothers her parents? That she doesn't eat right? Or what can happen because of a poor diet?

Focusing on the *results* and *how they feel about them* can help Chantel's parents. They don't say, "You must eat breakfast and dinner, or else!" Instead, they might say:

- **"When you skip breakfast, we worry that you'll be tired in school."**

Be Careful When You Feel Angry

Keep angry feelings out of your I-messages. Teens find it hard *not* to feel blamed for the anger. How would you feel if someone were angry with you?

Of course, you will feel angry with your teenager at times. But getting angry too often can lead to a struggle for power or revenge, or to displaying inadequacy. Your teen might feel threatened and quit talking to you.

To move away from anger:

- Give an I-message *before* you feel extremely angry. For example, your first feeling might be worry or disappointment. You could use an I-message with your teen at that point. That may reduce future angry feelings.

- Change your self-talk. The "Just for You" activity in Chapter 2 (page 45) gives you some ideas for doing this.

- Look for times to talk with your teenager when you are not angry.

I'm Extremely Angry—What Should I Do?

1. **Get away from your teen.** Leave the room. Go for a walk. Call a friend.

2. **Call a hot line.** If you are so angry that you are afraid you'll hurt your teenager, call someone for help right away. Hot lines have trained people who will help you get through an angry moment. Look in the phone book under "Crisis Numbers." Hospital emergency rooms often have numbers like this too.

3. **Seek help for yourself.** There are people who can help you learn to deal with anger. Call a counselor, social worker, or crisis center.

Anger is also discussed in Chapter 6, pages 121-24, "What About Anger and Violence?"

Be Ready to Listen

When you give an I-message about a problem, your teen might want to talk about it. Then you will want to use both reflective listening and I-messages.

One afternoon, Mom comes home from work a little early. She finds her 16-year-old son Sef and his girlfriend, Tasha, lying on the living room floor. Things are "hot and heavy."

Tasha is embarrassed. She jumps up, fixes her clothes, and leaves. Sef is flushed and angry. He says to his mom, "Why are you home early!" He stomps out of the living room.

Mom gives Sef time to calm down in his room. She makes supper and calls him to eat.

As they eat, she says to her son, "I was very troubled to find you and Tasha together like that today. I worry that you'll go too far. Tasha could get pregnant. And I think you're both too young to have sex." Sef says, "If I'm too young, how come my body wants to do it so bad?" Mom says, "It's confusing, isn't it?" Sef says, "Not to me! I <u>know</u> I want to do it!" "How does Tasha feel about it?" Mom asks. Sef answers, "She's scared . . . but I think she wants to." Mom says, "Sef, I know it's not easy, but there are <u>lots</u> of reasons to wait." Sef says, "I don't wanna talk about this anymore!"

This is not an *easy* conversation, but it *is* important. Even though Mom and Sef will need to talk more, this was a good start. Mom's I-message opened the door for Sef to talk to her. Mom listened to how Sef felt. She let him know her feelings too. She stayed respectful. Sef saw that Mom cared about him and understood some of his feelings. Mom also showed Sef that they could talk about tough problems. In Chapters 4 and 7, we'll look at other ways parents can talk with teens about sex.

Send Friendly I-Messages Too

Your teenager will love to hear friendly I-messages too:

- "It sure feels good to come home and find you cooking."
- "I noticed that you took out the garbage. Thank you."
- "I enjoy going to practice with you."

Sometimes, Just Ask

You can't use I-messages all of the time. If you do, your teen may quit listening. Sometimes a simple request is the best way to gain cooperation:

- "Would you please set the table?"
- "It would be a big help if you gave the dog a bath."
- "Please close and lock the windows when you go to bed."

How Can I Build My Teen's Self-Esteem?

I-messages show respect for you. They let you be honest about how you feel and what you want. They show respect for your teen too. They share your belief that your teen is willing and able to cooperate.

Parents' belief in teenagers helps teens believe in themselves. A way to show respect and belief in your teen is to be encouraging.

What Is Encouragement?

Encouragement is a skill to help teenagers grow in self-esteem. Self-esteem helps young people deal with life, have success, and get through problems. It helps them say "I can" and "I will." Encouragement is a way to show teenagers that they are

- **accepted**
- **capable**
- **loved**

Look at the words *encourage* and *discourage*. They both include the word *courage*, an important part of self-esteem.

An encouraged teenager has strong self-esteem. The teen has the courage to cooperate, try new things, and be responsible.

A discouraged teenager has little self-esteem. The teen doesn't have the courage to choose positive ways to belong.

An encouraged teenager has the courage to cooperate, try new things, and be responsible.

How Can I Encourage My Teenager?

Encouragement is based on the idea of respect. Teenagers need encouragement and respect all the time. Get in the "encouragement habit" to show that you:

- Love and accept your teen.
- Notice your teen's efforts.
- Appreciate your teen.
- Have faith in your teen.

Let's take a closer look at each way to encourage.

Love and Accept Your Teen

When we love and accept our teens, we see both their special qualities and their problem areas. We see their ups and their downs. Encouraged teens know that we don't expect them to be perfect. We accept our teenagers and value them the way they are.

Some parents think they need to keep pointing out what is wrong. They believe this will help young people improve. But this can be discouraging. What if your friend kept telling you what you did wrong? What if your boss criticized everything you did? This is how teenagers feel too.

All teens need love and acceptance no matter how they behave.

What if we treated our coworkers the way we sometimes treat our teen?

Nikki is 15. Yesterday, she told her dad she was staying overnight at Julie's. The truth was that Nikki went with Julie to a party. She smoked marijuana and drank. The police came. Nikki's dad had to get her at the police station.

Today at home, Nikki cries and says, "I'm horrible. I hate myself!" Dad says, "Nikki, what you did was wrong. But you aren't horrible. You made some bad choices. Let's talk about what you'll do about the lie. And, what can you do next time there's a party?"

Notice Your Teen's Efforts

Improvement takes time. Everything we learn is made up of small steps and efforts. The same is true for our teenagers. They are learning skills and ways to act. They are getting experience. This happens slowly, a little at a time.

Accepting Your Teenager

- **Think about a bad choice your teen has made.**

- **Think of a way to help your teen know that he or she is not a bad person.**

- **Think of a way to help your teen make a better choice.**

Marc is 16. He has been trying to find a job in a store. He has seen many "Help Wanted" signs and filled out lots of forms. But he has not had many interviews. No one has called him back to hire him.

Marc's parents think they know the problem. Marc wears messy, dirty clothes and a large earring. His hair is long and greasy. They might want to say, "If you cleaned yourself up and took out that earring, then someone might hire you!" But how will that help Marc?

Instead, Marc's parents decide to be encouraging. Dad asks, "Why do you think you haven't been hired?" Marc says, "I don't know! I've been on time for every interview. And I've been polite." Mom says, "Being friendly and polite seems to come naturally for you. And I've noticed that you've been careful to be on time." Marc says, "I think they're hung up on <u>looks</u>. They don't like my hair and earring." Dad says, "Maybe you could try a different 'look' for your next interview. See if that helps." Marc says, "I don't see why they can't take me the way I am." Mom says, "I know what you mean. I'd be more comfortable if I could wear jeans to work. But I can't. That's the way it is with some jobs."

Marc's parents have used encouragement and talked with him respectfully. In these ways, they're more likely to help their son. If Marc decides to make an effort to change, they can notice this too. How?

- They can point out small efforts and improvements along the way: "You were really careful filling out this application. That might help you get an interview."

- They can comment on what he is learning: "I see you're trying different clothes. A store manager will probably prefer clean slacks."

Appreciate Your Teen

Even though teenagers are becoming independent, they still need to be part of the family. They need a sense of belonging at home. When you say and show that you appreciate your teen, you encourage this belonging as well as cooperation.

Tomás is 14. When he has friends over, he is often mean to his little brother Diego. Mom wants to encourage Tomás to be kinder. She doesn't want to criticize. She has noticed that Tomás is often nice to Diego when the two of them are alone with the family. One night after Diego is in bed, Mom says to Tomás, "I appreciate how you read to Diego tonight. He really loves his big brother."

Mom decides to notice and appreciate Tomás's kindness to Diego as often as possible. She knows that might help Tomás think about the way he treats his brother when friends are around too.

Notice Learning and Improvement

Think about something your teenager is learning or improving in. Also think of efforts your teen has made. For example:

- Has your teen improved in a subject in school?

- Has your teen done something thoughtful?

Find at least one effort or improvement. Look for a chance to tell your teen that you have noticed.

Mom also thinks about other things Tomás has done lately that she appreciates: Tomás often sits and chats with Mom after school. He likes to help fix meals. He feeds and brushes the cat.

After only a few minutes, Mom finds many things she appreciates. She decides to start thanking Tomás for cooperating.

Another way to show appreciation is to notice what is important to your teenager. Ignoring a teen's interest is easy, especially if it has never been important to you. But our different interests are part of what makes each of us special. If you take the time to ask about an interest, your teen will feel appreciated. You might even discover a new interest for yourself.

Your teenager has strengths—positive qualities and talents. Notice and build on these strengths:

Jill's stepmom says to Jill, "Your hair always looks so nice. You have a talent for braiding hair." Jill says, "I learned a new way that would look really good on you. I could do yours that way." "I'd like that!" says her stepmom.

Have Faith in Your Teen

Teenagers need to know and see that parents believe they can succeed.

Malcolm, 16, is learning to drive. He has just finished his road training. Now he wants his dad to ride with him so he can practice for his license test.

The first time Dad and Malcolm ride together, Malcolm almost drives through a red light. He sees it and slams on the brakes. "Sorry!" he says, sounding mad at himself. Dad says, "You'll get used to watching for lights and signs as you get more experience." Later, coming into an alley, Malcolm almost scrapes the side of the car on a tree. He says, "Darn! Why is this happening?" "There's a lot to learn, Malcolm," Dad says. "Back up slowly and then straighten out the car."

Malcolm knows that his dad believes he can learn to drive a car. How? Dad tells his son that he can and takes the time to ride with Malcolm and teach him. This will help Malcolm feel able to try other things as well. It helps him tell himself, "I can do it."

Expectations are powerful. Our teens can sense what we truly feel and believe. Few teenagers will believe in themselves if we don't believe in them.

To show faith in your teenager, you may have to look at the big picture. Don't dwell on a mistake your teen made in the past.

Few teenagers will believe in themselves if <u>we</u> don't believe in them.

Instead, think about the many things your teen has learned to do right. Don't worry about a mistake your teenager might make. Instead, think about ways you can help your teen feel capable.

Remember, you have made mistakes in your life and survived. Your teen needs the chance to do this too.

Growing up is a process that takes years. When our teens were younger, they couldn't tie their shoes, read, or ride bicycles. Still, they did learn to do these things. Keeping this in mind may help you see that your teenager can learn many skills, over time.

A Word About Trust

You want your teenager to trust you. You also want to be able to trust your teen. This is a little different from having faith. At times, trust needs to be earned. This is especially true if your teenager has often lied to you or broken agreements.

You don't want to refuse to trust your teenager because of past mistakes. Yet you may not always trust your teen, either. You *can*, however, trust the process of learning and of building a strong relationship.

A simple way to help build trust is to think and act "as if." This expectation sends a powerful message. For example, act *as if* your teen will be responsible. Think *as if* your teen will cooperate.

If your teenager lies or breaks an agreement, the broken trust is an opportunity for your teen to learn and grow. It can be a chance for the two of you to work on your relationship. Be respectful and honest about your feelings. Listen to your teen's beliefs and feelings. Help your teen take responsibility for the consequences of breaking your trust. In Chapter 5, you'll learn more about ways to use consequences to help your teen.

What Is the Difference Between Praise and Encouragement?

Many parents believe they are encouraging teenagers when they praise them. They don't realize that praise can be *dis*couraging.

Praise and encouragement are not the same thing. Each has a different purpose.

Praise Is a Reward

Praise is a type of reward. Teenagers earn it. They might earn it by competing and winning. Maybe they earn it by being compared to somebody else. Praise from a parent gives a young person the *reward* of being valued by the parent.

There's a big varsity softball game after school. Tracy hits a home run. She scores two other runs. She pitches and strikes out three batters. Tracy's friend Allie has a bad game. She strikes out twice. She drops the ball on an important hit. But Tracy and Allie's team wins the game.

After the game, Dad says to Tracy, "Great game—thanks to you!" Tracy says, "It was sweet! Allie sure had a bad day though. I feel bad for her." "She should have concentrated more. You could teach her a thing or two!" Dad says. Tracy thinks, "What if I'd messed up like Allie? What would Dad think?"

What Does Praise Teach Teens?

With praise, teenagers learn to please others. There is nothing wrong with wanting to please someone. But with a lot of praise, some teenagers start to believe that they *must* please other people. They decide this is the *only* way to feel worthwhile.

Teenagers may also learn to want more and more praise. When parents do not praise them, they may worry and start to doubt themselves. They might even think that if they don't get praise, they are getting criticism!

Young people begin to see each activity as a contest to be "good at" or "bad at." They learn that one person can be "better than" someone else. They start to believe that competing to win the reward of praise is important.

Other teens may see praise as their parents' attempt to control them. In this case, praise can lead teenagers to rebel.

Encouragement Is a Gift

Encouragement is a gift. No one needs to earn it.

Encouragement can be given for effort or improvement:

A teen might be learning a tricky step for a dance line. A parent might say, "That looks smoother than it did last week."

It can be given as a way of noticing what is unique:

Later, the parent might say, "It's nice to watch you practice on the grass. I can see you from the window while I'm working."

Encouragement can even be given when a teen isn't doing well or is facing failure:

"When you got out of step, you faked till you could get back in. And you got back on track. Staying calm when you're nervous can be hard. That's a really important skill!"

Encouragement from parents helps teenagers feel valued for who they are. This helps them accept themselves and feel capable. It raises their self-esteem.

What Does Encouragement Teach Teens?

With encouragement, young people learn:

- **to appreciate their own special qualities**
- **to feel capable**
- **to feel worthwhile just the way they are**

Teens also learn that they can encourage themselves. They feel more self-confident. They are more interested in cooperating with others than in competing.

Praise Uses Words That Judge

"You're such a good kid!" This is not an easy thing to live up to. Hearing this, a teen might think, "Am I supposed to be good all the time? What if I'm not good? Am I bad? Am I worthwhile when I'm not doing what Dad wants?"

"You made the team—I'm so proud of you!" A young person might hear this as, "You make me look so good! You've pleased me by doing what I want." The teen might think, "I am worthwhile because I made the team. What if I didn't make the team? Would Mom be disappointed in me?"

Encouragement Uses Words That Notice

Encouragement focuses on how a teenager has helped. It looks at how the teen feels. With encouragement, a parent might say:

- "Thank you for introducing me to your friends at the mall."
- "You seem pretty proud of that!"

- **Teenagers need to learn to cooperate—not to be "better than" others.**
- **Teenagers need to feel accepted all the time—not just when they do something big.**
- **Teenagers need to learn to think for themselves—not to please somebody else.**

Using praise without encouragement will not help you meet the challenge of parenting.

- **Encouragement helps teenagers have faith in themselves.**
- **It helps them say "I can" and "I will."**
- **It helps them cooperate and care about others.**
- **It helps them grow to be self-motivated.**

Too much praise can be discouraging. Encouragement will better help you meet your parenting challenge. Most of the time, it is a better choice than praise.

Does this mean that you should never praise your teen? No. There are times when praise can be encouraging:

Your teen's choir just won first place in a singing competition. Their singing was wonderful. Would you tell your teen, "You must feel proud of how you sang"? No. You'd give your teen a big hug. You'd say, "Wow! What a performance! Way to go!"

We all like rewards. When young people work hard and accomplish something, offering our praise is fine. You will be a more effective motivator when you focus on the language of encouragement.

Use the Language of Encouragement

Encouragement has its own language. Here are some examples of words that encourage:

- "Thanks. That was a big help."
- "I trust your judgment."
- "That's a tough one, but I think you can work it out."
- "You really worked hard on that!"
- "You're getting better at geometry all the time."
- "You can do it."

The chart at the end of this chapter has more examples of the language of encouragement.

Thinking About Encouragement

Imagine your teen is running a race:

- **What you say at the finish line is praise.**
- **What you say <u>during</u> the race is encouragement.**

A Word of Caution

Sometimes parents say something encouraging but then add something discouraging. For example, a parent might say, "It looks like you really worked hard on that." A teen would feel encouraged. But what if the parent added phrases like these?

- "You really worked hard on that . . . I wish you'd do that more often."

- "I trust your judgment . . . so don't let me down."

- "You can do it . . . so quit complaining and get busy."

Statements like these give encouragement—and then take it away. The encouragement is canceled. The teen ends up feeling discouraged. Remember: You are building your teen's self-esteem, not making your teenager perfect.

Are There Other Ways to Be Encouraging?

Using helpful words and avoiding too much praise are two important ways to encourage your child. You can do other things too.

Act in Encouraging Ways

Don't encourage only with words. Our actions can be encouraging too.

A nod, a smile, or a "thumbs-up" sends a message of encouragement. So does listening without interrupting. So does a hug or a pat on the back.

You also show confidence in your teenager when you accept the teen's desire to try something challenging.

Kirk is a high school senior. He wants to go to Highview College, fifty miles away. He has a chance for a basketball scholarship. The coach has invited him to visit the college for a weekend. He'll stay in the dorm with two students. Kirk wants to go, but he's nervous about looking "young and stupid" to the college kids.

Kirk's parents want him to be able to go. They're worried about how nervous he is. Also, Kirk will be with older students. They're afraid he might get in a situation with drugs or alcohol.

They decide to help Kirk feel sure of himself. They listen to his feelings. They tell their son, "You are younger than the boys at Highview, but you're smart and capable. We know you'll be able to get along." They tell Kirk their concern about drugs and alcohol. Together, they discuss what Kirk can do if there's a problem. Kirk

---

Changing to Encouragement

Notice when you praise your teen. For example, notice when you say:

- **"You're such a good kid!"**

- **"You did a great job!"**

Think about different words you can use to encourage your teenager.

Teach Respect for Others

Self-esteem is extremely important. So is "people esteem"—feeling and showing respect for others. Truly respecting ourselves is hard if we don't respect others.

This means that teaching and showing respect is a way to encourage your teen. What are some ways to do this?

- **Help friends and neighbors.** Invite your teen to help too. The job might be large, such as helping someone move. It might be small, such as watering plants when a person is gone.

- **Look for opportunities to volunteer as a family.** Your teen's school might have a clothing drive. Help your teen collect clothes.

- **Use good manners.** Being polite is not old-fashioned. We all appreciate being treated politely. Make saying "please" and "thank you" to your teenager a habit: "Please clear your dishes before you leave." "Thanks for doing the grocery shopping."

- **Appreciate that people are different.** Our world is full of many kinds of people. We come from large families and small families. We come from different races and different places. We have different religions. We like different activities. By showing that you appreciate these differences, you may influence your teenager to appreciate them too.

Encourage Yourself

Things take time. Helping your child grow in self-esteem might take a long time. You are learning new parenting skills. This will take time too. You are changing how you speak and act. As you do, give yourself the gift of encouragement.

Remember That Your Teen Is Not You

Sometimes things will go well for your teenager. Then, feel happy for your teen rather than proud for yourself. Sometimes things won't go well for your teen. Then, show that you understand. You don't need to feel like a failure as a parent.

Set Realistic Goals

Don't set goals for yourself—or your teenager—that are sure to discourage you. If your teen is struggling in all subjects, don't set

Accepting and Valuing Yourself

Take some time to think about all the things you like about yourself:

- What is unique about you?

- When do you feel most capable?

- When are you happiest?

Keep a list in your purse or pocket. Add to it whenever you can. Let your list keep growing.

When you feel discouraged, read your list.

a goal of all A's. If you want to change your style of parenting, don't set a goal of learning every skill at once. Take life one step at a time.

As you work toward your goals, use self-talk to give yourself small doses of encouragement:

- "I stayed calm when Jack told me about what happened at the mall."
- "I didn't yell today."
- "I really listened to what Tuyen was saying."

Take some time to be good to yourself!

Be as Healthy as You Can

Working to stay healthy will help you handle your own feelings and your teen's behavior better. It also shows your teenager that taking care of one's health is important.

- **Eat balanced meals and get some kind of exercise every day.** This might be a daily walk or ten minutes of exercise at home. Invite your teen to join you.
- **Look for healthy things to do as a family.** Go walking or biking. Shoot hoops. Walk to do errands.
- **Use your valuable time wisely.** You can't say yes to every request for your time. Part of staying healthy is learning to say no.

Have Patience With Yourself

We often think of learning as a one-way trip that goes up, like a car climbing a hill. But learning doesn't happen like that. It is

For Your *Family*

Brainstorm ideas for having fun together. To brainstorm, have everyone suggest ideas. Stay open-minded. Sometimes ideas sound silly or impossible. Don't be quick to judge them. One "silly" idea might help someone think of another good one.

Choose at least one way to have fun together as a family. Plan what you will do and when you will do it. Then follow through. Have fun!

more like the ocean tide. When the tide comes in, it moves forward. Then it falls back and comes forward again. Each time it comes forward, the tide is a little higher on the beach.

The falling back can feel discouraging. Remember: Each time you move forward, you are ahead of where you were the last time.

You Have Taken Another Big Step

In Chapter 3, you have learned many ways to help your child and yourself:

- You have learned a way to tell how you feel without blaming or judging.
- You have kept thinking about how to have respect in your relationship with your child.
- You have seen how self-esteem and encouragement are connected.
- You have discovered the difference between praise and encouragement.
- You have found many ways to encourage your teen and yourself.

THIS WEEK

This week, find ways to encourage your teenager. Find as many ways as you can. Each time, notice:

- what happened
- how you encouraged your teen
- how your teen responded

Continue to stop yourself from talking without thinking. Instead, think of respectful ways to talk with your teen. Use I-messages and reflective listening as often as you can.

Encouragement STEP

This week, make a special effort to show acceptance to your teenager. Notice how this can help build your teen's self-confidence.

Be aware of times you want to judge or criticize. Find a way to show support instead. For example, you might say:

- **"I know you have trouble getting along with your government teacher. What do you think you can do to make your relationship easier?"**

- **"I know it was hard for you to visit your grandma in the nursing home. Thanks for making the effort."**

JUST FOR YOU

Humor Helps!

One of the best ways to help your teen and yourself is by having a sense of humor. In Chapter 2, you looked at ways to change your self-talk. Once you do this, you will be better able to find the funny side of things. It will help you feel more hope—and less anger. Where there's humor, there isn't room for anger.

Here are three questions to help you find and use your sense of humor:

- **"What if this were a funny TV show?"** TV sitcoms often show the funny side of parenting. If you're worried about a problem with your teen, ask yourself: Would this be funny in a sitcom? Why? What would I do next if this were part of a funny TV show?

- **"Why am I glad I'm not a perfect parent?"** Maybe you're glad there's room to grow. Maybe you're glad you can have a good cry. Maybe you're glad other parents aren't afraid of you. Maybe you're glad you can laugh with a friend about your mistakes.

- **"How can I be more playful?"** Relax. Act silly. If you find this hard to do, ask a friend to be silly with you. Notice how you feel when you start to act carefree and foolish. Then, when you are in a negative frame of mind, remind yourself of that more fun, silly feeling.

POINTS TO REMEMBER

1. You-messages put down or blame teenagers. I-messages tell how you feel without blaming.

2. To use an I-message, tell what is happening, what you feel, and why you feel that way. It uses these words:

   - When   "*When* you don't call,
   - I feel   *I feel* worried
   - because   *because* I don't know where you are."

3. Avoid using angry I-messages.

4. Building respect and trust takes time. Don't give up.

5. Encouragement is a skill to help teens grow in self-esteem. It shows that they are important, capable, and loved.

6. You encourage when you:

   - Love and accept your teen.
   - Notice your teen's efforts.
   - Appreciate your teen.
   - Have faith in your teen.

7. Praise is a reward that must be earned. It can teach teenagers to please others instead of thinking for themselves.

8. Encouragement is a gift. Everyone deserves it. It can be given for effort. It can be given when a teen is not doing well. And it can be given for just being.

9. Encourage your teen as often as you can.

10. You also encourage teenagers when you show respect for yourself and for others.

11. Setting realistic goals will encourage both you and your teen.

Chart 3

THE LANGUAGE OF ENCOURAGEMENT

Words that say "I accept you"	Words that say "I know you can"	Words that say "I see that you are working and improving"	Words that say "I appreciate you"
"You seem to like mysteries a lot."	"You can do it. You've made it partway already."	"You worked hard on that!"	"I needed your help, and you came through."
"How do you feel about it?"	"You're making progress."	"You're getting better at equations all the time."	"Thanks. That was a big help."
"I can tell you're pleased about it."	"I trust your judgment."	"Look at the progress you've made."	"It was thoughtful of you to do that."
"I can see you're not satisfied. What do you think you can do so you'll feel happier with it?"	"That's a tough one, but I think you can work it out."	"Looks like you spent a lot of time thinking that through."	"I really appreciate your helping me. It makes grocery shopping go faster."
"It looks like you enjoyed that."	"I need your help fixing this."	"I see you're moving along."	"I need your help planning the picnic."
"You did your best— that's all anyone can do."	"You'll figure it out."	"You may not feel you've reached your goal, but look how far you've come."	"You have skill in _____. Would you do that for the family?"
"I enjoy your sense of humor."	"Knowing you, I'm sure you'll do fine."		"I really enjoyed our game. Thanks."
"It's nice that you enjoy school so much."			

Developing the Courage to Be Imperfect

You are almost halfway through *Parenting Teenagers*. Sometimes, parents feel guilty at this point. You might feel as if you have been raising your teenager in the "wrong" way. Be patient with yourself. Remember your parenting challenge:

- **to encourage your teenager to be healthy, confident, cooperative, and independent**
- **to build a strong, lifelong relationship with your teenager**
- **to help your teenager grow to be a responsible adult**

Here is one more idea to help you with this challenge. Rudolf Dreikurs had an idea he called the *courage to be imperfect.** With the courage to be imperfect, you quit worrying about what happened in the past. Instead, you focus on what is happening today. You can:

1. Encourage your teenager to make efforts, not to expect perfection.

2. See mistakes as part of learning—not failures. Everyone makes mistakes.

3. Work at being helpful—not better than others.

4. Do what you can and accept your own efforts.

5. Take the next good step.

6. Make small changes—don't try to be a whole new you.

7. Value yourself.

8. Get to know your own strengths and good qualities.

9. See parenting as a challenge to be met—not a problem to overcome.

By reading this book, you send a clear signal that you are willing to consider new ideas. It is a sign of growth. Know this, and encourage yourself as you continue to progress!

*Dr. Rudolf Dreikurs, an internationally known psychiatrist, originally developed the idea of the courage to be imperfect.

CHAPTER FOUR

Encouraging Cooperation *and* Solving Problems

As parents, we often face challenges with our teenagers. We can guide our teens to do two things:

- take responsibility for their own problems
- cooperate with others to solve problems

How Can I Deal With Problems?

In Chapter 1 you learned how to decide who owns a problem. The person who owns the problem is responsible for solving it. Does this mean you shouldn't help your teen solve his or her problem? No. Sometimes you will want to help. But if the problem belongs to a teenager, then the teen is in charge of it.

Sometimes the Teen Owns the Problem

Let's look at two problems owned by teenagers.

Boyfriend Trouble

Rita is 16. She and her boyfriend, Darnel, are in the living room. Dad, in the kitchen, hears arguing. Rita says to Darnel, "That was so mean! How could you say that about me?" She sounds hurt and angry. But Dad knows that Rita owns the problem in her relationship with Darnel.

What Can Dad Do?

- For now, Dad can and should do nothing. He doesn't go to the living room and ask, "What's wrong?" If the noise bothered Dad, his rights would be disrespected. He'd own the problem. If Rita and Darnel started throwing things or if someone could be physically hurt, Dad would also own it.

- Later on, if Rita wants Dad's help, he may want to listen and offer his ideas. But he can't take on the problem for himself. Rita is still in charge of solving her problem.

Study Habits

Malik is 15. He has a history test Friday. On Monday, he says to his mom, "I'm worried about my test. Will you help me review this week?" Mom says, "I'll be glad to help tonight or Wednesday night."

On Monday night, Malik chooses to do something else. On Wednesday he goes to a basketball game. Now it's Thursday night. He says to his mom, "Can you review my history with me now?" Mom says, "Not tonight, Malik. I have a meeting." Malik whines, "But you promised to help me!"

Malik's schoolwork is his job. He didn't take help when Mom could give it. He also didn't study all week. This problem belongs to Malik.

What Can Mom Do?

- Right now, there is nothing Mom can—or should—do to save Malik. The consequence of a bad grade is his. If Mom skips her meeting to help him review his history right now, what will Malik learn? That he doesn't need to be responsible; that he doesn't need to respect Mom's time; that Mom can save him from his own bad choices. This could become a pattern for other issues besides schoolwork.

- At another time, Mom can talk to Malik about study habits. She might say, "For a test, studying a little each day helps. Would you like to talk about some ideas for getting organized?" If Malik wants to talk, he and his mom might have ideas to share.

- Mom can think about the goal of Malik's behavior. If Mom feels annoyed, Malik may want attention. Mom would be wise not to give Malik the payoff he wants. If she feels like giving up, he may be displaying inadequacy. In that case, Malik's problem is Mom's problem too. A teen who displays inadequacy is extremely discouraged. Mom would need to find ways to encourage her son.

Sometimes the Parent Owns the Problem

Now let's look at a problem the parent owns.

"Mouthing Off"

Jessica is 14. Her mom told her she can't go on overnights or hang out at the mall. Now Jessica has started to be "mouthy" to her mom. Last night Jessica swore at her mom and said, "You can't tell me what to do!" Jessica uses bad language about her mom to a friend on the phone. Mom hears her and feels hurt. She feels angry too. Mom has a right to be treated with respect. So Mom owns this problem.

What Can Mom Do?

- Mom can think about Jessica's goal. Does Jessica want revenge? Then Mom can avoid feeling hurt. She could do something Jessica doesn't expect. She might ignore the rudeness for a while.

- Mom can use an I-message to tell Jessica how she feels: "When you swear at me and call me names, I feel discouraged because it seems you don't respect me."

- Mom can use reflective listening to give Jessica feedback: "You sound really angry with me. Can we talk about it?" If Jessica is willing, she and Mom can talk the problem through.

- Mom can give Jessica a choice: "You may stay in the kitchen if you can be respectful. Otherwise, please leave the room. You decide."

Some parents are extremely upset by swearing. In this case, saying nothing and walking away are often best. This can be a powerful response.

When sisters and brothers fight, they usually own the problem.

Sometimes, the Parent and Teen Own the Problem Together

Here are two problems owned both by the parents and by the teens.

Underage Drinking

Doug is 14. He went to a school dance. The chaperons checked his breath and found he'd been drinking. They called his parents. Doug's parents own the problem of their son's drinking. Drinking at 14 is illegal and dangerous. But Doug is learning about balancing freedom and responsibility. He is responsible for his own actions. So he owns this problem too.

What Can Mom and Dad Do?

- Doug's parents can think about Doug's goal. He may be seeking attention and acceptance from friends. He may be seeking power and excitement by taking risks or acting big. Mom and Dad may want to help Doug find excitement that isn't illegal.

- Doug's parents must let Doug accept the consequences the school sets for drinking. That might mean that he is suspended from school for a while. Or it might mean he can't play in sports or take part in music or plays. Sometimes schools work with the local police when drinking is involved. Doug may have to go to juvenile court or do community service.

- It is important for Doug's parents to look at their own drinking. What kind of example are they setting for their son?

- Doug's parents also need to look at how much or how often Doug is drinking. Was this a one-time act? Or is Doug drinking often? The answers to these questions will lead Mom and Dad to different ways of working on this problem with their son. They may need to get some professional help.

Chapter 7 talks more about teenage drinking and getting help. See page 143–47, "What About Drinking and Using Other Drugs?"

Teen Sex

Anya is 17. When her mom washes Anya's coat, she finds condoms in the pocket. She talks to Anya. Anya tells Mom that she has had sex with her boyfriend several times. Mom is shocked and upset about this. She'd always hoped that Anya would wait to have sex until she was much older.

Mom knows that Anya will make up her own mind about having sex. But Mom has values she wants to keep teaching Anya. She also worries that Anya will get pregnant. She worries that Anya could get a sexually transmitted disease (STD). This problem belongs to both Anya and her mom.

What Can Mom Do?

- Mom can use I-messages to tell Anya how she feels. She might say, "I feel really worried to know you're having sex. There are lots of ways you could be hurt."

Thinking About Who Owns the Problem

Think about a problem you have with your teen. Ask yourself:

- Are my rights being disrespected?

- Could anybody get hurt?

- Is someone's property threatened?

- Is my teen unable to take this responsibility?

Decide who owns the problem—you, your teen, or both of you.

- Mom can use reflective listening to understand Anya's feelings. Anya might say, "I won't get hurt! Derek and I love each other!" Mom could answer, "You feel safe because you know Derek loves you." Or Anya might say, "You don't have to worry. We're using condoms." Mom could answer, "You seem to feel sure that a condom will protect you." If Mom stays respectful and caring, Anya may be willing to keep talking. Listening can help Mom learn many things. She might learn that Anya feels grown up, that Anya wants to please Derek, or that Anya has mixed feelings.

- Mom can keep using I-messages to help Anya understand how Mom feels. At the same time, she needs to realize that Anya may decide to keep having sex. If this is the case, Mom needs to do what she can to make sure Anya knows how to keep from getting infected or pregnant. She has to talk about all the consequences of STDs and pregnancy. She needs to talk about how Anya might feel later if she and Derek break up.

Alcohol and sex are two areas of big challenge for parents and teens. Use them as chances to listen, respect, and cooperate.

How Can My Teenager and I Solve Problems Together?

Deciding who owns problems helps you know what to do. It helps your teen become independent and responsible. If you—or you and your teen—own the problem, you need to take action. If the problem isn't yours, sometimes letting your teen figure it out is better. Sometimes helping your teenager solve it is better.

You've already learned many things to do when there's a problem. You might ignore it. You might listen for feelings or use an I-message. You can make sure your teen sees the choices and the possible consequences. Another encouraging way to solve a problem is to talk it through with your teen. You take the time to listen, talk, and agree about a way to solve the problem. This is called *exploring alternatives*.

An encouraged teenager has the courage to cooperate, try new things, and be responsible.

"Talking It Through": Five Steps for Exploring Alternatives

No matter who owns a problem, exploring alternatives has five steps:

1. **Understand the problem.** Make sure the problem and people's feelings are clear to both you and your teen. Use reflective listening. Ask questions that help you understand. Explain the problem clearly and respectfully. State your own feelings with I-messages: "When _____, I feel _____ because _____."

2. **Brainstorm ideas to solve it.** To brainstorm, ask your teen for ways to solve the problem. Suggest your own ideas too. You can help by saying, "What might happen if you _____?"

   These ideas are the *alternatives*. Stay open-minded for this step. Sometimes ideas sound silly or impossible. Don't be quick to judge them. One "silly" idea might help you or your teen think of another good one. For now, just list *any* ideas that come up.

3. **Discuss the ideas.** Now is the time to consider the ideas. Read your list. Discuss the ideas, treating your teen as your equal. Both you and your teen should feel free to "try on" the different ideas. If you don't agree with an idea, state your view respectfully. Don't say, "I'm sure that idea won't work." Instead, you might say: "I'm concerned that sticking to that plan will be hard for you."

4. **Choose an idea.** Pick an idea you both can accept. If the teen owns the problem, the teen picks the idea. The parent would become involved only if the idea was dangerous to the teen or others. If the parent and teen own the problem together, both would need to agree on the idea.

5. **Use the idea.** Agree to test the idea. Decide together how long to use it. Plan enough time to give the idea a fair test. Often a week is a good test period.

   Also, set a time to discuss if the idea is working. If it isn't, explore alternatives again. Or try out another idea from the first time you brainstormed.

As you explore alternatives, work to see and hear feelings—both your teen's and yours. This will help you understand each other. It will help you both stay focused on solving the problem.

Use Open Questions

When talking with your teen, you will ask questions. Ask *open* questions, not *closed* questions. Closed questions call for *one* answer only—there is no room for discussion. Some closed questions can be answered only yes or no. Other closed questions blame or criticize:

- "Do you think we're made of money?"
- "Don't you think you should study tonight?"
- "Why did you do that?"
- "Are you ever going to grow up?"

Open questions invite your teenager to keep talking. They show respect. They show that you want to listen:

- **"How could you earn money?"**
- **"What makes the biology labs so hard?"**
- **"How do you feel about that?"**
- **"What would you rather do?"**

Asking Questions

Think of a problem you have with your teenager. To understand how your teen views the problem, think of some open questions. Use these words to start your questions:

- **Where?**
- **When?**
- **What?**
- **Who?**
- **Which?**
- **How?**

Practice asking open questions. Work to keep your face, body, and tone of voice respectful. Show respect for yourself and your teenager.

Put yourself in your teen's place. How would you feel to be on the receiving end of too many closed questions?

Where have you been? Why didn't you call? Do you think I have nothing better to do than sit up and worry? Don't You think You owe me an apology?

Exploring Alternatives: Two Examples

Let's look at two examples of exploring alternatives. Each example is for a problem you've already seen: Rita's trouble with Darnel and Mom's problem with Jessica.

Rita's Problem: Boyfriend Trouble

Rita and her boyfriend, Darnel, have been arguing a lot. Dad has noticed, but he hasn't gotten involved. Tonight, Rita comes and sits by Dad as he watches TV. She sighs and looks sad. Dad senses that Rita wants to talk. He decides to offer to explore alternatives.

Steps for Exploring Alternatives

1. **Understand the problem.**
2. **Brainstorm ideas to solve it.**
3. **Discuss the ideas.**
4. **Choose an idea.**
5. **Use the idea.**

1. **Understand the problem.**

Dad says, "You look pretty glum." Rita says, "I'm okay." She doesn't sound okay at all. Dad says, "Your eyes seem to say you're unhappy. But maybe you'd rather not talk about it." Rita says, "It's Darnel. I just don't know what's going on with him." Dad waits. Rita goes on, "I mean, he's so nice when we're alone together. But then he treats me like dirt in front of his friends."

Dad sees that Rita knows she has a problem. She seems to want to talk some more.

2. **Brainstorm ideas to solve it.**

Dad says, "That's pretty embarrassing, huh?" "It *hurts!*" Rita exclaims. "I asked him how he'd feel if I did the same thing to him." Dad says, "So you've talked to Darnel about how you feel?" Rita says, "I try to talk to him, but he acts like I'm making a big deal out of nothing."

Dad asks, "Do you want to kind of practice talking to him with me?" "No," says Rita. "I don't need to practice! I talked to Maria, and she thinks I need to tell him to hear me out. Oh— I don't know!" Rita sighs again. Dad is careful. He sees that Rita is thinking of ideas her own. He believes he can help best by listening. He says, "You sound pretty discouraged."

Rita says, "I am. I'm thinking about breaking up with him. The trouble is, it's so nice when it's just the two of us." Dad asks, "What if you just took a few days 'off' from Darnel, without breaking up?" Rita says, "I hadn't thought of that."

3. **Discuss the ideas.**

Dad and Rita keep talking. Dad mainly listens and asks questions. In this way he helps Rita sort out her feelings. If Rita wanted to stop talking at this point, that would be fine. The problem is Rita's—Dad doesn't need to ask her to agree to anything. But Rita doesn't stop. She keeps talking with Dad.

4. **Choose an idea.**

Rita says to her dad, "I think I'll call Maria and see what she thinks about taking a few days 'off.'"

5. **Use the idea.**

Dad says, "I'll be glad to talk some more if you want to." Rita goes to call Maria.

Later, Dad might ask Rita what she decided to do. Or he might not ask her. Deciding when to ask and when to stay quiet can be tricky. By listening and staying respectful, Dad has shown Rita that he is there if she wants to talk. He has helped her see that people can discuss problems and think about different ways to solve them. He has shown her a calm, thoughtful way to do this. Without labeling it as exploring alternatives, he has shown his daughter how to do it.

Mom's Problem: Jessica's Rudeness

Jessica has been rude to her mom for several days now. She swears at her mom and yells at her. She calls her mom names. This problem belongs to Mom. She decides to explore alternatives with Jessica.

1. **Understand the problem.**

Mom waits for a quiet time. She and Jessica are home alone. Jessica isn't busy with schoolwork or TV or the phone. Mom is feeling calm, not angry. She says, "Jessica, you seem very angry with me lately. What's going on?" Jessica snaps, "You control of my life!" Then she calls Mom a bad name.

Mom stays calm. She says, "I'd like to talk about this with you. But when you swear, it's hard for me to stay respectful. Could we agree to talk calmly for just a few minutes?" Jessica glares at her mom. Mom waits quietly. Jessica says, "Fine. I'll be calm. But I can't believe you don't know that I'm the only one of my friends who *can't* go to the mall on weeknights, and who *can't* go on overnights, and who *has* to be off the phone by ten, and who has so many *rules* it's like I was eight years old!"

Mom says, "You really feel I'm being unfair. I didn't know you felt this way." Jessica says, "If you paid any attention to me at all—apart from noticing when I'm breaking your stupid rules—you'd know how I feel!"

Now Mom knows what the problem is. Jessica feels Mom's too strict. She also feels that Mom doesn't care about her.

2. **Brainstorm ideas to solve it.**

Mom is careful not to feel hurt and angry. She doesn't want a battle of revenge. She stays calm and says, "Let's talk about the rules. Do you think you should be able to go to the mall every day?" Jessica swears and says, "There you go again! No, I don't even *want* to go every day!" Mom says quietly, "Swearing and being rude seem to tell me that you don't really want to work this out." Jessica stares angrily but says nothing. Mom asks in a friendly voice, "What goes on at the mall?" Jessica says, "Nothing special. But lots of kids hang out at the food court."

Jessica begins to see that Mom is willing to listen to her feelings. Mom stays calm, but she doesn't accept swearing or rude talk. Mom tells Jessica why she worries about overnights. Jessica says that she feels left out when she has to miss them. She also tells Mom that her friend Sally often can't use the phone before ten o'clock at night. Her brother has it tied up using the computer.

3. **Discuss the ideas.**

Mom and Jessica keep talking. Mom says she doesn't feel right about the idea of hanging out at the mall. But she is willing to agree to overnights once in a while. Jessica thinks Mom is being unfair about the mall. But she would like to go on overnights. She would like to be able to talk to Sally on the phone after ten at night. Mom agrees that she may be too strict about some things. She tells Jessica that she wants to be treated respectfully.

4. **Choose an idea.**

After more talking, Jessica and Mom agree that Jessica can go on one overnight this month, as long as an adult is there. They also agree that she can talk to Sally until as late as 10:30 if her homework is done. Mom says, "I'll expect you not to swear or yell at me, Jessica. To keep the privilege of talking until 10:30, you'll need to get off the phone without me nagging. Do you agree not to swear and yell at me? I'll agree to stay respectful too." Jessica agrees.

5. **Use the idea.**

Jessica and Mom decide to test the idea for one week. At the end of the week, they'll talk about how things are going.

Mom's problems with Jessica aren't just going to go away. But exploring alternatives has helped her begin to build a better relationship with her daughter. Jessica has seen that Mom won't get involved in battles for power or revenge anymore. She has seen that Mom is willing to listen. She now knows that respectful talking will help her get more freedom. She's seen that she needs to take more responsibility too.

When Talking Is Hard

Sometimes there seems to be no way to solve a problem. You or your teen may be extremely angry. Or you may see things completely differently. Maybe both of you believe that you are right. Maybe you are having trouble being patient. You may think, "This is hopeless. We'll never get anywhere!"

When you have a *conflict* like this, don't give up or start taking complete control. Instead, use these ideas to help you find a way to cooperate.

It takes two people to "agree" to fight.

Stay respectful. You know that respect is important. When you stop showing respect to your child, you are not respecting yourself, either.

Dad and his daughter are arguing and interrupting each other. To get back on track, Dad says: "When we both talk at once, we can't hear each other. Let's listen and respect each other's feelings. Why don't you speak first—I'll listen."

Talk about the real problem. In a conflict, getting carried away is easy. Then you lose sight of the problem.

You want your daughter to do her chores. An argument starts. You get angry and think to yourself, "I need to put her in her place!" These feelings tell you something important: You have lost sight of the problem about chores. The real problem seems to be about who's in control.

You stop yourself. You take a deep breath and say to your daughter: "It seems we're both trying to be the boss. How will that help us solve this problem?"

Admitting that we are part of the problem is okay. That gives young people a way to admit their own part in it too. It will help both you and your teen find a solution.

Agree not to fight. In a conflict with your teen, you have an agreement. You haven't talked about this agreement, but it is there: *You have "agreed" to fight!*

Take a step back. Look to see if a hidden "agreement" is keeping you from solving the problem. If it is, you could say: "It looks like we've both decided to argue instead of try to solve the problem. I'm willing to get back on track if you are. What do you say?" Keep your voice and face friendly.

Wait and talk later. At times, you and your teen will seem unable to find an acceptable idea. If this happens, you may want to return to step 2 and brainstorm again. Or you may decide to stop exploring alternatives until both of you have had a chance to think things over.

If the problem needs immediate attention, you may have to make the decision on your own. Offer your teen a chance to talk about it again at another time: "It seems we aren't able to solve this problem, so I'll make the decision for now. We can talk about it again in a few days to see if we can find a solution together." It may happen that your teen will refuse to talk at all. In this case, too, you may have to make the decision.

Write it down. Sometimes writing down the agreement is helpful. Post it on the refrigerator or have the teen keep it until it is reviewed.

You and your teen could also sign the agreement. That shows mutual respect and says, "We are serious about this."

Look for how you are alike. Sometimes, recognizing that your similarities contribute to a problem is helpful. This can be hard when you are in conflict, but consider these examples.

Two verbal people might want the last word in a disagreement.

Two sensitive people might feel hurt if harsh words were exchanged.

At these times, put yourself in your teen's shoes—and recognize that they fit! Recognizing your similarities may help you see things differently. It may help stop the conflict.

How Can Family Meetings Help My Relationship With My Teenager?

One more good way to build cooperation among everyone in a family is to have a regular family meeting.

Some people wonder if a family meeting is worth the effort. They say, "Why have a meeting? We already see each other every day!" They think, "Meetings are for work, for church, for committees—not families!"

If you ask someone whose family has regular meetings, you will hear that family meetings:

- **Help families feel like a "team" where people help each other.**
- **Give everyone a chance to share good feelings and have fun together.**
- **Teach children and teenagers about respect and problem solving.**
- **Help families stop hitting and yelling.**
- **Give children and teens a place they know they'll be heard.**

Ling is 14. His sister Mahti is 11. Mahti comes crying to her dad in the kitchen. She says, "Ling made me quit using the computer. He always makes me quit. I was in the middle of a game." From the living room, Ling hollers, "Dad, I've gotta do my homework!"

Dad just got home from work. Supper is late. He feels too busy and crabby to talk this through with his children. So Dad goes with Mahti into the living room. He says to Ling and Mahti, "Let's talk about this at the family meeting. Write it on our list on the refrigerator."

Dad doesn't get angry and hit or yell. Ling and Mahti know their problem won't be ignored. Even before the meeting, this family is helped by knowing there will be a chance to solve the problem.

Guidelines for Family Meetings

Getting into the habit of family meetings takes time. Making the meetings work takes effort. Here are some ideas to help you.

Meet at a regular time. A regular time might be once a week. Plan to have the meeting last from twenty minutes to an hour.

Make a list of topics. Some people call this list of topics an *agenda*. Post it on the refrigerator. Then people can add to it during the days before the meeting. This helps you deal with the things that are important to each person in the family.

Plan the time. At first, you will need to be in charge of this. Look at the meeting list. Decide how much time makes sense for each item on the list. Stick to the time limits.

Take turns being the leader. The leader reads the meeting list and keeps things on track. Still, letting each person in the family have a chance to lead is important. Younger children will need help to do this. That's okay.

The family meeting gives teens a place they know they'll be heard.

Take notes. Write down the agreements and plans made in the meeting. These written notes are the *minutes*. Take turns doing the job of note-taking. Find a place to post the notes so everyone can read them. Some families put them on the refrigerator near the

A Family Meeting Plan

1. **Share good things that have happened.**

2. **Read the notes from the last meeting.**

3. **Talk about "old business"— things from the last meeting.**

4. **Talk about "new business"— things people want to talk about at this meeting.**

5. **Plan something fun to do.**

6. **Summarize. Say what people have agreed to.**

Using a Job Jar

One way to take turns is by using a job jar:

- **Talk together about all the jobs that need to be done each week.**

- **Write them on slips of paper and put them in a jar.**

- **Each week, draw jobs out of the jar.**

next meeting's agenda. Ask teens and older children to read the notes to younger children who don't read yet.

Let everyone take part. When talking about something on the list, let the young people in the family speak first. This helps them feel responsible.

- If someone hasn't talked, ask, "What do you think?"

- If someone talks too much, stay respectful. You could say, "It sounds like this is important to you. We need to hear how everybody else feels about it."

- If someone is not showing respect, use an I-message: "When I hear name-calling, I get concerned that we won't be able to cooperate."

Limit complaining. Lots of complaining can turn meetings into gripe sessions. This won't solve problems. It won't help families enjoy each other. If complaining is a problem, ask, "What can we do about it? How can we solve the problem?" Remember to listen for feelings and to share yours. When problems arise, explore alternatives.

Cooperate to choose chores. To start, you might want to volunteer for a chore no one likes. You might say: "I'll clean the cat box or the bathroom. Which should I do?" As time goes on, expect others to do some of the unpleasant chores too. Some families take turns doing different chores. Others use a job jar.

Do what you agree to do. Stick to agreements until the next meeting. If people want to change the agreement, they can do it then. Children, teenagers, *and* parents are expected to do what they agree to do.

What if *you* forget and break an agreement? What if one day you don't have time to do something you agreed to? Tell your family you are sorry. Say you will work to do a better job. A teenager might sometimes forget or not have time too. No one is perfect.

If broken agreements continue, make a "work before fun" rule: Before people do fun activities, their chores need to be done. The rule applies to parents as well as teens and younger children.

Take time for fun. Meetings are a good way to solve problems and choose chores. But that's not all they are for. To add fun to meetings, talk about good things. Thank each person for some help given during the week. Ask each person to do the same. Ask people to talk about what is good for them right now. This sets a positive tone. It also teaches your children to encourage other people—and themselves.

At the meeting, plan together to do something you all enjoy. You might plan to make home-made pizzas together on Sunday night. Maybe you'll plan to watch a football game together on TV. Some families spend time having fun together right after the meeting. Respect people's busy schedules, though. Teenagers may have other plans for after the meeting.

Family Meetings Work for All Kinds of Families

Family meetings are for all families—one parent or two, one child or many, and stepfamilies too.

Some families have two parents, but only one who wants to have family meetings. That is okay. You can have meetings without the other adult. Maybe, after a while, the other adult will see how well the meetings work and will decide to join in. If not, keep up the meetings anyway. They will still give you a chance to help teens and younger children cooperate and enjoy each other.

Single-parent families. If you are a single parent, family meetings can help you too. One thing is different for some single-parent families: talking about problems that have to do with the parent who is not there. Children and teens need to be able to talk about these problems. But the family meeting is not the place to do that. The family meeting is to help the people who live together get along better.

If your teen wants to talk about the other parent, do it at another time. You might say, "You want to talk about your weekends at Mom's. Right now we're talking about things that happen here. Let's talk about Mom after the meeting."

Is there an exception to this suggestion? Yes. Whenever the actions of the adult not in the family directly affect the family, those actions can be discussed in the meeting. An issue might be changed or missed visitations, for example. Limit discussions to the issue only. Don't blame the other adult.

If you talk about the other parent after the meeting, you can still listen for feelings and give feedback. Keep following the steps you have learned for exploring alternatives.

Two-person families. If you are a single parent with one child, you may be thinking, "Why should I start having family meetings? My teenager and I are together at home all the time."

The family meeting does many things that daily togetherness will not always do. It lets you set aside time to talk about problems. It gives you time to focus on good things too. Family

Finding Time for Meetings

Your family is busy. Find the time to meet by making a chart of everyone's activities. Fill in everyone's schedule for the week. This will help you find or make time when all family members are free for a family meeting. Here are things to talk about in family meetings:

- **kids' activities**
- **allowances**
- **errands**
- **chores**
- **rules when friends visit**
- **weekend plans**
- **phone use**
- **TV and movies**
- **homework**
- **family computer use**

meetings help you and your teen become closer and cooperate more. No matter what size, a democratic family will benefit from regular family meetings.

Stepfamilies. Stepfamilies need meetings as much as any other families. In a stepfamily, people may not have lived together for long. If you are in such a stepfamily, you might want to try this plan for family meetings:

- Always start family meetings on a positive note, not in response to a crisis or an argument.
- Start with issues that you think will be easy to talk about, such as family fun. After a few of these meetings, start talking about harder issues. You might talk about chores. You could talk about one problem that seems to be troubling the kids.
- Keep issues that aren't about *your stepfamily* out of your meetings.

You Have Taken Another Big Step

In Chapter 4, you have looked at ways to help your teen cooperate:

- You have seen ways to cooperate to solve problems you—or you and your teen—own. You have also seen ways to help your teenager own and solve problems.
- You have learned five steps to follow to solve problems with your teen.
- You have seen how family meetings can help your family work and grow together.

Encouragement
STEP

Think about some of the ways you and your teenager are alike. For example:

- **You both might like music.**
- **You both might like having lots of friends.**
- **You both might feel cranky when you first wake up.**

Think of as many ways you are alike as you can. If you have a problem with your teen, use what you have thought about. Look at the problem from your teenager's point of view.

THIS WEEK

If you think your teen is ready, practice exploring alternatives. If you decide to explore alternatives for a problem between you and your teen, have in mind:

- when you will talk
- how you will begin
- what changes you are willing to make
- what you will do if agreement is not reached

JUST FOR YOU

Seeing Things Differently

Can you look at a situation in different ways? Doing this helps change your response to disappointing events. For example, you may see your teen as stubborn, refusing to cooperate. Can you also see the teen as determined? Can you see that a teenager seeking power also wants to make decisions? If so, you are seeing your teen in another way. You are finding something positive in negative behavior.

Think of several difficult situations. Then ask yourself:

- How do I usually see this? What do I believe? How do I feel? How does my usual reaction create problems?

- Is there another way to view this situation? How might that view change what I feel and do?

Look for ways to create another way to see a situation.

For Your *Family*

Invite your family to start having regular meetings. Agree on a time for the first meeting. Before you meet, read pages 82-85 again. When you meet, explain the purpose of family meetings:

- **to share good feelings**

- **to have fun together**

- **to make plans**

- **to talk about problems and help each other**

Then ask your teen and other children what they would like to talk about. Keep the first meeting short. Agree on a time for the next meeting.

Don't expect to have a "perfect" meeting. You are just getting started! The most important thing is for everyone to feel that his or her ideas are important.

Good luck!

POINTS TO REMEMBER

1. When there are problems with teenagers, someone "owns" the problem. Sometimes the parent owns it. Sometimes the teen owns it. Sometimes the parent and teen both own the problem.

2. To decide who owns a problem, ask yourself:
    *   Are my rights being disrespected?
    *   Could anybody get hurt?
    *   Is someone's property threatened?
    *   Is my teen unable to take this responsibility?

    If the answer to *any* question is yes, you—or you and your teen—own the problem. If the answer to *every* question is no, your teenager owns the problem.

3. The person who owns the problem is responsible for solving it. Sometimes parents will want to help teens solve their own problems.

4. When there is a problem, you can choose to ignore it, use reflective listening, use an I-message, give a choice, or work on solving it by exploring alternatives.

5. To explore alternatives, follow these five steps:
    *   Understand the problem.
    *   Brainstorm ideas to solve it.
    *   Discuss the ideas.
    *   Choose an idea.
    *   Use the idea.

6. When you talk with your teen about a problem, use open questions that begin with:
    *   Where?
    *   When?
    *   What?
    *   Who?
    *   Which?
    *   How?

7. When you are angry and in a conflict with your teen:
    *   Stay respectful.
    *   Talk about the real problem.
    *   Agree not to fight.
    *   Wait and talk later.
    *   Look for how you are alike.

8. Regular family meetings help all families cooperate to solve problems and have fun together.

Chart 4

EXPLORING ALTERNATIVES

Step	When teen owns problem	When parent, or parent and teen own problem
1. Understand the problem.	"Sounds like you're very hurt when the others laugh at you. What do you do when they laugh? What do they do when you get angry?"	"When you come home late, I get very worried because something might have happened to you." "You're annoyed because you think I'm overprotective?"
2. Brainstorm ideas to solve it.	"What are some other things you could do when they laugh?"	"How can we solve this so I don't worry and so you feel in charge of your life?"
3. Discuss the ideas.	"What do you think about the first idea—laughing with them?"	"How do you feel about calling if you're going to be late?"
4. Choose an idea.	"Which idea do you think will work best? What do you think will happen if you do this?"	"It seems we're in agreement on this idea."
5. Use the idea.	"Are you willing to laugh with them just to see what happens? It may take them a while to get used to a new response from you. Would you be willing to do this several times? Shall we talk about it on _____?"	"As I understand it, you'll call me if you're going to be more than fifteen minutes late. Is that the way you understand it? What would be a fair consequence if you decide not to call? If I slip and get angry with you, what do you think should happen? Shall we do this for a couple of weeks and then talk about how it's going?"

CHAPTER FIVE

Using Consequences *to Build* Responsibility

You have learned many ways to build your relationship with your teenager. In this chapter, you'll begin to learn about *discipline*. You will learn a style of discipline that makes sense—one that will help you guide your teen to cooperate and make responsible decisions.

Are Discipline and Punishment the Same Thing?

Discipline and punishment are *not* the same thing. Using punishment and rewards to try to control behavior won't help young people become independent and responsible. In Chapter 1, page 3, we talked about what teenagers learn from rewards and punishment:

- Rewards teach teens to get something—not to cooperate.
- Punishment teaches teens to resent and fear us. It can hurt the relationship we want to have.
- Punishment often stimulates revenge.

What Is Punishment?

Punishment is a style of relationship. It includes many things, like the following.

Threats, yelling, and put-downs. Sometimes the threats are carried out. Sometimes not. Lots of yelling may make things worse. If we yell a lot, teens may start to pay attention *only* when we shout. Or they

Here's what you will learn . . .

- **Discipline helps your teenager become more responsible.**

- **Discipline is a way to guide your teen in making choices and decisions.**

- **Consequences are a method of discipline that fits the behavior and makes sense to the teen.**

- **Using consequences shows respect for all family members.**

may stop listening altogether. Put-downs and name-calling aren't good for anybody—parents or young people. When teens hear yelling and put-downs, they often use them too.

Taking things away and grounding. Often parents punish teenagers by grounding them. Many times the grounding has nothing to do with what the teenager did. That doesn't make sense. Often, too, the *way* the parents take away something isn't respectful.

Hitting. A parent might hit a teenager out of anger. Hitting may be a last try at controlling the teen. Sometimes the parent feels like there's no other way to get the teen to behave. Hitting hurts both the teen and the parent: The teen feels unloved. The parent feels guilty. The teen also sees that hitting is a way to solve a problem or get power.

What Is Discipline?

Discipline is not a single act or statement. It is a process that takes time. Discipline helps teenagers:

* Take charge of their own lives by making decisions.
* Learn from the consequences of their choices.

How Can I Discipline My Teen?

In earlier chapters, we looked at many ways to show respect and encourage cooperation. Here we will focus on *choices* and *consequences*. Let's look more closely at how to give choices and let your teen learn from consequences.

Give Choices and Opportunities to Make Decisions

Many parents are afraid to let young people make their own decisions. They worry that teens will take too much freedom—and not enough responsibility. We need to give teens the chance to make choices and decisions *within limits*. As teens grow, they still need limits. But those limits need to change as the teenagers become more mature and responsible.

Thinking About Discipline

Think of a time you corrected your teenager without punishing.

* **What did the teen do?**
* **What did you do?**
* **Why do you think your teenager decided to behave better?**
* **How did you and your teen feel about it?**
* **How could you use that kind of discipline for other problems with your teen?**
* **If you had yelled at, hit, or grounded your teen, how would things have been different?**

What are some choices and limits parents can offer teens?

- Teens can have an allowance or earn money from a part-time job. They can use their money to buy clothes or special things they want. (Not illegal or harmful things, of course.) The limit is the amount of the allowance or paycheck.

- Teens can make their own decisions about which classes to sign up for in school. The limits are the graduation requirements, college-entrance requirements, and available courses.

- Teens can choose which activities they want to take part in at school, church, or other organizations. The limits are what the programs offer and what the costs will be.

- Teens can choose which TV shows to watch. The limits are the amount of time and the content of shows that the parent and teen agree to.

Other choices are less easy to limit. Yet teens make these choices too:

- Teens choose their friends. Parents can't choose friends for their teens but can work out limits. These might cover where teens may go or how late they may stay out.

- Teens choose how they'll behave in school, in the car, on dates, or at social events. Parents can set or work out limits such as curfews, car rules, and doing what's legal.

Will teens always make wise choices? No. But choices give teens the *experience* of making decisions. Teenagers need that experience. They learn from the results of the choices they make. In other words, they learn from consequences.

Let Your Teen Learn From Consequences

A consequence is what happens because of a choice or decision the teen has made.

Some Consequences Just Happen

Consequences that just happen because of an action are called *natural consequences*.

- If Tove doesn't eat breakfast, she'll be hungry in school.

- If Brian stays up until 3 A.M. and has to get up for school at six, he'll be tired.

Teens learn from the consequences of choices they make.

Some Consequences Need to Be Created

Some natural consequences aren't safe. Also, many behaviors aren't covered by natural consequences. In those cases you will need to create *logical* consequences.

> Chandra just got her driver's license. Her dad sees that Chandra drives too fast in the apartment parking lot. The speed limit is ten miles per hour. That rule is important because children often play in the parking lot.
>
> Dad says to Chandra, "Driving over ten miles per hour isn't safe. You could hit a child or another car. You can use the car if you agree to stay within the speed limit. Otherwise I'll know you've decided not to drive the next day. It's up to you."
>
> Chandra agrees to drive within the speed limit. A few days later, Dad sees her driving too fast again. That night he says to Chandra, "I see you've decided not to drive tomorrow."

Consequences Aren't Punishment

Here are some ways consequences are different from punishment:

- They show respect for both you and your teen.
- They fit the misbehavior.
- They are about behavior.
- They are about now and the future—not the past.
- They are firm and friendly.
- They allow choice.

Consequences Show Respect for Both You and Your Teen

Consequences respect *both* you and your teen.

> Your 14-year-old son is listening to loud music. You are trying to sleep. You don't yell at him to turn it down "or else." You say, "Sounds like you're really into that music. But I need my sleep. Please turn the volume down, or use the headphones."

Consequences Fit the Misbehavior

Consequences make sense. They "fit" the misbehavior.

> Jon is 13. He leaves a mess in the kitchen. His dad doesn't say, "No football game for you on Friday night!" The football game has nothing to do with leaving a mess. Instead, Dad says, "I like to come home to a clean kitchen. Please clean it up. Otherwise, I won't be able to fix dinner."

The Keys to Helpful Discipline

- Show respect for your teen.
- Expect your teen to cooperate.
- Give choices and opportunities to make decisions.
- Apply consequences.

Consequences Are About Behavior

Consequences are for bad choices—not "bad" kids. You may have heard the phrase "Separate the deed from the doer." Consequences help you do that. The misbehavior—not your teenager—needs to be fixed! Consequences tell your teen, "I don't like what you're doing, but I love you."

Without asking, Renée wears her mom's shoes to the homecoming bonfire. It rains, and the shoes are ruined. Mom doesn't say, "You had no right to take my shoes without asking! You're going to have to work a lot of hours to earn the money you owe me!" Instead, she says, "How will you replace the shoes, Renée?"

If a consequence doesn't make sense, what lesson will be learned?

Consequences Are About Now and the Future—Not the Past

Consequences deal with now and the future. They are not about the past.

Lauren is 17. She asks her mom, Barb, if she can have a birthday party for her friend. Barb doesn't say, "No you can't have a party. All you did last time was leave a big mess. And some of your friends were drinking." Instead, Barb says, "You can have a party as long as you're willing to clean up afterward and there's no drinking."

Consequences Are Firm and Friendly

Consequences are firm and friendly. They show respect and caring.

Misha is 14. He asks his grandma to drive him to the library to use the computers there. They agree she'll pick him up at 8:00. She gets there right at 8:00. She waits and waits. At 8:30, Grandma goes into the library. She looks all over and finds Misha in the computer room. He's playing a game with some friends. Grandma doesn't say, "Misha, I've been waiting half an hour! How can you be so thoughtless? Come to the car right now!" Instead, Grandma says, "Please come out to the car right now."

The next day, Misha wants a ride to the library again. Grandma says, "I waited outside the library a long time last night. I'm not willing to do that again tonight. Tomorrow, we can see if you feel ready to keep our agreement."

Logical consequences fit the misbehavior: Each consequence will be different.

Consequences Allow Choice

With a choice, the teen has some control.

On Saturday morning, Dad says to Lucas, "You can vacuum before you go to Susan's or after, as long as you're done by 4:00, when our company's coming. You decide."

How Can I Set and Use Consequences With My Teenager?

There are four steps in using consequences. We'll look at the steps one at a time.

1. Identify the Goal

When your teen misbehaves, use consequences. For the consequences to be effective, you first need to think about the goal of the misbehavior.

Attention

When a teen seeks attention, it's best to avoid giving that attention on demand.

Sam is 13. He loves to have someone new to play his guitar for. Dad tells Sam, "I know you like to play for people. But tonight I'm having a meeting here. It won't be okay for you to play your guitar. If you'll agree to do something quiet on your own, you can stay inside."
Sam needs to learn when and where sharing his music is acceptable. His dad also needs to pay attention to him at other times, when he isn't expecting it. For example, Dad can show appreciation when Sam gives the dog a bath. He might ask Sam to play his guitar at specific, reasonable times.

Power

When a teen seeks power, the best consequence is having no one to fight with.

When Rashida doesn't get her way, she tries to force her parents to give in. She gets angry and tells them they're being unfair. Today Rashida's mom and dad decide not to fight <u>or</u> give in. When Rashida starts her angry shouting, her parents simply leave and go for a walk. Rashida is surprised and confused. She doesn't <u>have</u> her audience.

A teen who wants power also wants some control. At other times, when Rashida isn't trying to have a power struggle, her parents can ask for her opinions and her help. They can offer her chances to make reasonable choices.

If your teen seeks revenge, use consequences instead of feeling hurt. They can help you focus on building respect and trust.

The school notifies Ann's parents that Ann is failing in school. They feel embarrassed and hurt. Good grades are important to them. Ann knows that. At first, they try to force Ann to work. They ground her. They tell her she can't watch TV or use the phone until her grades are better. But Ann's grades don't improve.

Ann's parents decide to visit a family counselor. The counselor thinks that Ann is failing as a way of getting even. She suggests that they decide to let Ann be responsible for school. Instead of focusing on school, they can work on improving their relationship with Ann.

Backing out of her school life is hard for Ann's parents. But they decide to make the effort. At first, the grades don't improve much. But Ann and her parents begin to get along better. They start to talk and enjoy each other. Respect begins to return. They start to have fun together. Slowly, Ann's schoolwork begins to improve too.

Ann's parents went to a counselor. Something like that can help when parents are out of ideas. The counselor helped them step back and think about how they were responding to Ann. The counselor helped them change their response. Over time, leaving the problem alone and focusing on their relationship helped Ann improve.

Punishment rarely does what parents want it to. That is especially true with teens who seek revenge. Teens sometimes see consequences as punishment. *When* a consequence is used can be important.

Fourteen-year-old Jackie is angry at her dad, Bill. She storms off to her room. As she passes the lamp, she kicks it with her foot. The lamp crashes to the floor and breaks. Bill doesn't give Jackie a consequence right now. He knows it would sound like punishment. Jackie could get more angry. The war of revenge might continue.

Instead, Bill waits until later that night. He says to Jackie, "We need to talk about fixing or replacing the lamp."

Displaying Inadequacy

Creating consequences aren't helpful for a teen who displays inadequacy. The teen has given up. In that case, don't give up, don't criticize, and don't pity. *Do* give as much encouragement as possible. Focus on what your teen *can* do. When you see progress or effort, say so. In that way, you *can* help your teen gain confidence to try in other areas.

Trading Jobs

Trading jobs can be a highly effective consequence when chores become a problem. Don't use this approach as a weapon, though. Use it simply as a means to share chores fairly. Be sure the jobs you trade are equal. Otherwise you may be setting the stage for revenge.

2. Decide Who Owns the Problem

If your teen owns the problem, you probably won't need to create consequences. They will already be there. As long as the consequences aren't dangerous, you don't have to step in:

- If Tyrone stays up too late, he'll be tired the next day.
- If Kip misses the school bus, she'll have to find another way to get to school.

When you own the problem, you may decide to create consequences. Many parents struggle with the chores not being done. "Job trading" is a good way to use consequences here.

At a family meeting, Thai agrees to collect and put out all the recycling. He agrees to shovel the walk if it snows. Mom agrees to take care of the plants, the dog, and the laundry. She says to Thai, "If you find you can't do a chore, come talk to me. I'll be glad to trade one of my jobs for yours."

On recycling day, Thai leaves for school without collecting and putting out the recycling. He says nothing to Mom. Mom sees that the job is not done, so she does it. That night, Mom says to Thai, "I had to put out the recycling this morning. What job of mine would you like to do tonight? You can water the plants or walk the dog. You decide."

Thai says, "I have plans tonight!" Mom says, "Neither job will take long. There's no need to cancel your plans." Thai says, "Okay. I'll walk Kiko." Then he says, "It looks like it's gonna snow tomorrow. But I have an away game and I won't be home till late." Mom says, "If you're not able to shovel, I'll do it. Then you can take care of your laundry on Saturday." "Okay," says Thai. He doesn't sound happy. Mom says no more.

What if Thai isn't willing to discuss trading jobs? This approach could still keep Mom out of conflict. She doesn't have to try to force Thai to do anything. She can just skip those chores she does for Thai. These might be laundry, driving him places, or cooking. In a week or two, she can discuss chores with Thai again. That will give him another chance to cooperate.

3. Offer Choices

When using consequences, offering choices is important so that teens can learn to make decisions. If you do this, keep in mind that *either choice is a good decision*. It's a learning experience. Be ready to accept whatever the decision may be.

- **"Either pick up the things you left in the family room, or I'll put them in a box in the storage room to get them out of the way."** Your teen may leave the things in the family room. That's not one of the choices. Then you'll have to get the box and put your teen's things in it.

Negotiating Consequences

Whenever possible, work out consequences together with your teen. In other words, negotiate the consequences. Teenagers are more likely to accept consequences they have helped decide. You might ask:

- "What would you do if you were the parent?"
- "What would be fair?"
- "Can we talk about this for ten minutes?"
- "What do you think of this idea: _____?"

Be sure to negotiate before problems occur. Don't wait until a problem or power struggle is occurring.

At times, negotiation won't make sense. Maybe the problem is too small. Maybe it's too serious. Maybe there aren't many possible choices. Maybe your teen refuses to help or chooses an impossible consequence. In these cases, set the consequence. There will be many other chances to negotiate with your teen!

- **"Either slow down, or stop the car and I'll drive."** If your teen slows down, will you be comfortable in the passenger seat? Don't make this offer if speed isn't the only problem.

- **"Your friends can sleep here as long as you're all willing to be quiet after midnight."** Expect cooperation. But be prepared to take the friends home—or to call their parents to come get them.

- **"I'm willing to wash only the dirty clothes I find in the hamper."** This tells your teen: "You may put your clothes in the hamper or not." Follow through by washing the clothes in the hamper. Don't go around collecting dirty clothes!

4. Follow Through

If your teen chooses the consequence, the decision has to stand for the moment.

Marta is 14. She's looking forward to a weekend retreat with her youth group. She also has a term paper due the day after the retreat. Two weeks ago, Mom told Marta, "You can go on the retreat as long as your term paper is finished. If it's not done, you'll have to stay home." Marta agreed.

On the Friday afternoon of the retreat, Marta says to Mom, "I didn't quite finish my paper. I still have to write one section. But I can do that Sunday night." Mom says, "We agreed you'd be finished before the retreat." Marta says, "But Mom, they need me at the retreat. Mr. Canelli won't understand if I don't come. And I have a skit to help with. It'll be all messed up. They'll be so mad!"

Mom stays firm but friendly. She says, "It's too bad the paper isn't finished, Marta. That was our agreement."

There may be an opportunity to change a decision at a later time, though.

Marta stays home, unhappy. On Friday night she stays in her room and finishes her paper. She doesn't come out to talk to Mom at all. On Saturday morning, the phone rings. Marta answers it. Then she runs to the kitchen and says to Mom, "It's Mrs. Canelli. She didn't go with the rest of the group last night. She's driving there today. She said I could ride with her. Can I go?" Mom asks, "Is your paper all done?" Marta says, "Yes, I finished last night." Mom says, "Hurry and pack!"

Marta made her choice. Mom followed through. Marta accepted the consequence and finished her paper. Now she has a chance to go to the rest of the retreat. There's no reason for Mom to say no now. Saying no at this point would be punishing Marta.

Consequences: Two Examples

Let's look at two examples of using consequences.

Summertime Messes

Tammy is 15. It's summertime. She plays softball with a city league. The team practices every day at 4:00. Tammy is home alone until Dad gets home from work at 3:30. Then Dad takes her to practice. Each day this week Dad comes home to a mess. The kitchen is full of dirty dishes and half-eaten food. Games and clothes are all over the floor. Dad feels angry. He feels like he does all the work and Tammy does nothing but play. He tells Tammy, "You need to clean up around here!" But Tammy still doesn't. The problem is becoming a power struggle. Dad thinks about the problem. His rights are being disrespected. He owns this problem.

On the way to practice, Dad uses an I-message. He says to Tammy, "When I come home to a mess, I feel discouraged because I have to clean a mess I didn't make." Tammy says, "Dad—it's vacation. I need some time off from work!" Dad doesn't argue. He stays respectful and says, "I need some time off too. If I have to clean up and drive to practice, that's too much. I'll tell you what: I can clean up or drive you to practice. Which do you prefer?" Tami sighs, "Oh all right, I'll clean up. It's hard to find another ride."

The next day when Dad comes home, the mess is gone. Dad drives Tammy to practice. A day later, things are starting to get messy again. Tammy says, "Time to go to practice!" Dad says, "I see you've decided to find someone else to drive you." "Dad!" shouts Tammy. "I cleaned up <u>almost</u> all of it!" Dad says nothing more. He begins to pick up in the kitchen. Tammy makes some phone calls, but no one is home. "The coach'll be mad, and it'll be your fault!" she says angrily. Dad still says nothing. He follows through and stays out of the power struggle.

Stolen Shoes

Carlo is 14. His mom notices that Carlo is wearing fancy new shoes. Mom knows that Carlo can't afford such expensive shoes. She asks him, "Where did you get those shoes?" Carlo says, "Toby gave them to me. He got new shoes and didn't want these anymore."

Mom can see that the shoes are new. Carlo is lying. She feels angry about that. She says, "Carlo, if that's true, you'll have to give the shoes back. Please call Toby and tell him you're going to give him back his shoes. Or should I make the call?" Carlo scowls. He says, "Okay—I lied! I took the shoes from the store. I tried them on and then walked out when the clerk went to help somebody else." Mom glares at Carlo. Carlo shouts, "Don't look at me like that! It's not my fault you're too cheap to buy me shoes like everybody else has!"

Steps for Using Consequences

1. **Identify the goal.**

2. **Decide who owns the problem.**

3. **Offer choices.**

4. **Follow through.**

Mom feels hurt and angry. She feels worried too. She thinks about Carlo's goal. Her feelings tell her he may have more than one goal. He clearly is seeking peer acceptance by taking shoes like "everyone else" has. He wants to get even with Mom for not buying him more expensive shoes. Mom decides that Carlo wants peer acceptance, power, and revenge. Mom knows that trying to get even with Carlo will just make him want more revenge. So Mom decides to refuse to fight or get even. She needs time to think, so she says, "I'm too upset to talk right now. I need a few minutes alone. Then we'll talk about this some more."

Mom thinks about who owns the problem. Carlo stole something that wasn't his. It involves someone else's property—the store's. Mom and Carlo both own the problem of Carlo's stealing the shoes.

Mom thinks about what choices she can offer. The choice is not if, but <u>how</u> the shoes are returned to the store. Carlo must return them. Mom says, "You need to return the shoes to the store. I can drive you over tonight. Would you like me to come in with you, or wait outside? It's up to you."

Carlo must accept the consequence of what he did. But this choice can help him. If he needs support, Mom will give it. At the same time, Mom has shown she still trusts him enough to let him go by himself. Mom's message is strong. It tells her son, "You must take the consequence for what you did. I know you can do the right thing."

Mom takes Carlo to the store. He decides to go in without her. When he comes back, he tells his mom that the manager wasn't friendly at all. "He told me I was lucky I didn't get caught. They call the police if they catch someone stealing. And he told me not to come back to the store again until I'm sixteen." Mom stays quiet. She doesn't say, "Well, I hope you've learned your lesson," or "Next time I hope you'll know better!" Saying those things would turn the consequence into a punishment.

Even if stores in your community have different policies on shoplifting, this example shows a respectful, logical way to negotiate consequences—here and in many adult-teen situations.

Guidelines for Using Consequences

Here are some guidelines for using consequences.

Be Both Firm and Kind

Strict and *firm* do not mean the same thing. To be strict is to show that you are the boss. To be firm is to show that you expect cooperation and respect for yourself. Your voice and body language show your kindness. You show firmness by following through with consequences.

If You're Having Trouble

If you find it hard to use consequences:

- **Show an "open" attitude. Give the choice and accept your teen's decision.**

- **Use a friendly tone of voice that shows goodwill.**

- **Make sure the consequence fits the misbehavior.**

- **Be sure that you mean to give a choice.**

- **Stay consistent and follow through.**

- **Add more time to the consequence if the teen continues to misbehave.**

Practicing How to Say It

When you give a consequence, your purpose is to let your teen learn. Three things are important:

- **your tone of voice**
- **your body language**
- **the words you choose**

Think about a problem with your teenager and respectful words for giving a choice. Practice saying the words in front of a mirror.

Talk Less, Act More

Teenagers quit listening when parents talk too much. The best time for talk is when you and your teen are on friendly—or at least respectful—terms. When you use consequences, talk as little as possible as you follow through with action.

Don't Fight or Give In

Set or negotiate limits. Let your teen respond to them. Then accept your teen's decision. You aren't in a contest, and you don't have to "win." The goal is to help teenagers be responsible for their own behavior.

Use Respectful Words

When giving a choice, use a friendly and helpful tone:

- "You can rent movies if you agree not to get any that are violent."
- "I can call Ted's dad about the party, or you can ask Ted to have him call me. Which do you choose?"
- "I'm expecting a call shortly. Please use the phone for only five minutes or wait until later."
- "If you take the car, please see that no one smokes in it."
- "You can bake cookies as long as you leave the kitchen as clean as you found it."

Respect the Choice

Your teen may choose the consequence to see if you mean what you say. When that happens, respect the choice. Simply say, "Your behavior tells me you've made your choice," or "I see you've decided." Keep your voice matter-of-fact. Keep your face and body matter-of-fact too.

Make It Clear When There Isn't a Choice

Often parents offer a choice they don't mean. One way they do that is by saying "Okay?" Asking "Okay?" is giving a choice:

- "Everyone will be sober at this party—okay?" Your teen may decide that not staying sober is one of the choices.
- "No friends here while I'm gone—all right?" Your teen may decide, "That's not all right with me."

If there truly is no choice, don't hint that there is. That just sets the stage for problems. Instead, be clear about what you expect:

- "I expect that everyone who comes to the party will be sober."
- "You may not have friends in while I'm gone."

Focus on Positive Behavior

Focus on positive behavior as soon as possible after correcting misbehavior. Maybe you've used consequences because your teen stayed out all night without calling home. Now look for positive things you can encourage in the future: kindness to a younger brother or sister, helpfulness around the home, efforts in schoolwork or a sport.

Don't Worry About What Others Think

Sometimes teenagers push limits in front of their friends—or yours. This is a way of testing you. Following through is important. Standing firm is not easy when there's pressure from other teens or adults. But the message to your teen is strong. Your teenager sees that your limits are clear and consistent.

Sometimes you might be embarrassed by your teen's behavior. You might think it shows something bad about you. But teenagers have minds of their own. They won't always act as we wish they would. When they don't, it's not always because of us.

Stay Calm

Yelling, nagging, or making threats turn a consequence into punishment. Keep calm. Be both kind and firm. Show respect for yourself and your teen. If you do get angry and find it hard to stay calm, *wait*. Say nothing. Get away to a different room to cool down. If you can't leave the room, tell your teenager, "I'm too angry to talk right now. We will need to talk about this later." Take deep breaths and think about a way to give a choice.

The goal of discipline is to teach self-discipline.

Our teenagers won't always act the way we wish they would. We don't need to be embarrassed.

Respect the Other Parent or Parents

Adults in a family don't always agree on discipline. If that is true in yours, each parent needs to deal with the teen in his or her own way. Fighting about discipline won't help your teenager. Teens usually adjust to each parent's way. Show cooperation and respect for the other parent as best you can. If you're separated or divorced, agreeing with the other parent's discipline may be hard. As long as the teens aren't abused physically or psychologically, accept the system.

However, if the other parent hits or yells, that is *abuse*. Abuse harms the teen. You can't cooperate with abuse. If you suspect abuse, call upon others for help.

Stepchildren may not always accept discipline from a stepparent. Unless problems happen between a stepparent and stepchild, discipline is best left to the other parent—the one the teen is used to dealing with. As relationships improve, the stepparent can move into an equal discipline role with that parent.

Be Patient

Consequences work, but they take time. You are changing your old ways. A new and maybe very different system is beginning. Your teen may be testing your limits. Stay patient with yourself and your teenager. Slowly, you will see progress.

You Have Taken Another Big Step

In Chapter 5, you have learned a way of discipline that makes sense:

- You have looked at the differences between punishment and discipline.
- You have learned a way to set limits and give choices.
- You have seen that you can discipline your teen by showing respect and firmness.
- You have thought about choices and decisions that are appropriate for your teen.
- You have seen that following through is important.
- You have practiced ways to look and speak so that your teen feels respect instead of anger.

THIS WEEK

Choose one discipline problem to work on. Don't start with the hardest one! Think of consequences you could use. Think of what to say and do when you offer the choices. Be consistent, friendly, and firm. Follow through with your consequences.

Encouragement
STEP

Notice when your teen makes a sincere effort. Give encouragement. For example:

- **"You spent a lot of time doing that."**
- **"It feels good to make progress."**
- **"Thank you for remembering our agreement."**

Notice especially when your teen cooperates.

JUST FOR YOU

The Rights of Parents and Teens

Parents and teens have rights. Centering your life on your teenager is not fair to you or your teen.

As a parent, you have the right to:
- friendships
- privacy
- time for yourself
- respect for your property
- a life apart from your children

Your teenager has the right to:
- a safe and loving home
- friendships outside the family
- privacy
- respect for property

These rights can be summed up in one phrase: *respect for each other.*

This week, look for ways to hold to your rights. What will you do to show respect for your teen's rights?

For Your *Family*

Continue with family meetings. Discuss consequences for broken agreements. When discussing consequences, say, "We all forget sometimes. What should happen if someone forgets an agreement we've made?" Children and younger teens may come up with ideas that are punishments, such as spanking or grounding. Other teens may say, "I'm not gonna forget." If that happens, explain that you're not comfortable with that solution. Brainstorm more ideas.

For chores, many families decide to set a rule of "work before fun." Before people do fun activities, their chores need to be done. The rule applies to parents as well as children and teenagers.

POINTS TO REMEMBER

1. Discipline helps teenagers learn to be responsible. It helps them learn self-discipline.

2. The keys to effective discipline are:
   - Show respect for your teen.
   - Expect your teen to cooperate.
   - Provide choices and opportunities to make decisions.
   - Apply consequences.

3. Instead of giving orders, set limits and give choices.

4. A consequence is what happens because of a choice the teen makes. Consequences are a way to set limits and give choices. Consequences:
   - Show respect for you and your teen.
   - Fit the misbehavior.
   - Are about behavior.
   - Are about now—not the past.
   - Are firm and friendly.
   - Allow choice.

5. To use consequences:
   - Identify your teen's goal.
   - Decide who owns the problem.
   - Offer choices.
   - Follow through.

6. Consequences aren't helpful for a teen who displays inadequacy.

7. Some guidelines for using consequences are:
   - Be both firm and kind.
   - Talk less, act more.
   - Don't fight or give in.
   - Use respectful words.
   - Respect the choice.
   - Make it clear when there is no choice.
   - Don't worry about what others think.
   - Stay calm.
   - Respect the other parent or parents.

8. Be patient with yourself and your teenager.

Chart 5

CONSEQUENCES AND DAILY ROUTINES

Time of day	Activity or problem	Who owns problem?	Possible choices (Use respectful tone)	Consequences
Morning				
School days	Getting up on time	Teen (if walks or takes bus)	Provide alarm clock. Teen sets clock and gets up or is late.	If late, deals with school. If misses bus, walks.*
		Parent (if drives teen)	"If you're ready by _____, I'll drive you to school. If not, you'll need to find your own way."	If misses ride, has to deal with school if late.*
	Breakast	Teen	Teen makes own breakfast or doesn't eat.	If misses breakfast, goes hungry.
Weekends	Messy room	Teen and parent	Agree on time room will be cleaned and what "clean" means.	If room not cleaned, teen doesn't go out until room cleaned. Or parent uses job trading.
After school	Homework	Teen and parent	Agree on when homework is to be done, such as before or after dinner.	If homework not done, next day teen does it before dinner.
				If becomes power struggle, parent backs off and lets teen take school consequences.
	Friends in home when parent gone	Parent	"You may wait till I'm home to have friends over or I'll arrange for someone to watch you."	Arrange for an adult to watch teen.
	Teen late for meal	Teen	Agree on mealtime in advance.	Teen prepares own meal and eats alone.
Evening	Teen doesn't do dishes as agreed	Parent	"I can't cook in a messy kitchen."	Parent lets dishes pile up, does not cook.
	Too much TV	Parent	Agree on amount of TV. Let teen choose programs within limits.	If teen breaks limit, turn off TV.
	Too much time on phone	Parent	Agree on length of calls or way to pay for second line.	If teen talks longer than agreed, parent hangs up phone. Teen pays all or part of second line charge.
	Teen wants to play sports	Teen	Teen can play as long as keeps grades up to level parent and teen agree to.	If grades slip, teen doesn't play.
	Drinking and driving	Teen and parent	Parent sets limit in advance: No drinking.	Teen owns problems of hangover or trouble with police. Parent owns safety issue. Teen's driving rights suspended for a set time. If drinking becomes a problem, parent seeks help for teen.

*If you think your teen won't go to school, ask for the school's help.

CHAPTER SIX

Deciding **What to Do: Part 1**

So far you have learned to use these skills to help your teen make responsible choices:

- **Identifying the goal** helps you decide how to respond.
- **Reflective listening** is helpful when your child owns the problem.
- **I-messages** help you tell how you feel when you own the problem.
- **Exploring alternatives** is helpful no matter who owns the problem.
- **Giving choices** and opportunities to make decisions depends on who owns the problem.
- **Encouragement** is the cornerstone of your relationship with your teen. Use it as often as you can.

How Can I Decide What to Do?

The skills you use will depend on the situation. Sometimes you will use only one, sometimes all. Here's an example.

Here's what you will learn . . .

- The approach you use depends on the situation.
- To decide what to do, ask yourself what the teen's goal is, who owns the problem, what your purpose is, and how you can best help.
- With schoolwork, your job is to help your teen be ready and able to succeed.
- You can use your skills to help your teen deal with everyday problems.
- Using your skills can help your teen avoid some serious safety problems.

Carmen's School/Work Choice

Over the summer, 16-year-old Carmen had a part-time job. She liked having money of her own. Now that school is starting, she wants to keep working. Her mom believes school is more important than a job. She wants to be sure that Carmen has time to study.

At the family meeting, she talks to Carmen about the job. She says, "I understand you want to keep working after school starts." Carmen says, "Yeah—you got a problem with that?" Mom uses an I-message: "With both school and a job, I worry that your grades will slip." Carmen says, "My grades'll be fine." She adds sarcastically, "Thanks a lot for all your faith in me."

Mom stays respectful. She uses reflective listening. "Sounds like you feel hurt—it seems like I don't believe in you. But I do. I'd like to help you figure out a way to make it work." "I don't need your help!" says Carmen. "I can handle it by myself!" Mom decides to let Carmen be responsible. So she sets reasonable limits. She says, "Okay. You can keep your job as long as your grades don't slip from last year. And as long as you don't work later than nine o'clock on school nights." "Okay," says Carmen.

The second week after school starts, Carmen tells her mom, "I have to work until ten tonight. But you don't have to come get me. My boss said she'd drive me home." Mom says, "We agreed you wouldn't work later than nine on school nights." Carmen says, "I know! And I asked her not to schedule me. But we're shorthanded. Mom, it's a job! I can't always choose my hours!" Mom says, "You feel I'm being unreasonable because I want you to stick to our agreement?" Carmen says, "Yeah. That's not how things work when you have a job." Mom says, "Carmen, you'll need to stick to our agreement. I'm willing to let you work late this week, since your boss is counting on you. But that's it. How can you work it out with her so you aren't there past nine again?"

Carmen rolls her eyes. "Mom—what if she fires me?" Mom asks, "You worry that she'd fire you, even though she's shorthanded?" Carmen says, "Well, I guess she does need me right now. One reason I have to stay late is so she can finish adding up receipts while I handle the phone. Maybe she'd let me help her total the receipts. I could do a subtotal up to nine o'clock . . . But it seems like she'd be helping me, instead of me helping her."

Mom says, "That's an idea, though. You could suggest it. And I wonder if you could ask some other workers if they'd switch shifts with you." Carmen and her mom brainstorm a few more ideas. Carmen decides to explain that she can't work after nine and ask how she could help before then. She also decides to see if her friend's older brother would like to apply to work some later hours. Mom says, "Let me know how it goes." They agree to talk about it again at the family meeting next week.

At the next family meeting, Carmen reports that her boss was understanding about the late hours. Things seem to go well for several weeks. Then a midquarter school report comes in the mail. Carmen is getting a D in geometry. Mom says to Carmen, "You seem to be having trouble with geometry." Carmen says, "That test was so hard! Nobody got higher than a C on it!" Mom says, "Carmen, we agreed you could keep working if your grades didn't slip. You're going to have to quit the job until you get that D back up where it should be." Carmen gets mad. She shouts, "That's <u>not</u> fair! I've been doing fine all quarter. I forget to study for a few weeks and then get a D on one lousy test, and you want to take away my job!" Mom stays calm. She says, "You may go back to work once you've improved your grade." Carmen says, "That's so stupid! Do you think my boss will hire me back after I quit on her?" Mom stays respectful. She says, "You are angry because you think I'm being unfair. But we have an agreement." She doesn't say any more. Carmen keeps yelling, so Mom leaves the room.

What Did Mom Do?

Mom needed to use all of the approaches to deal with Carmen's behavior. You can see that she used them a little at a time.

First, Mom used an I-message. Her I-message let her state her feelings respectfully. It showed Carmen that she was willing to talk about the problem, not give orders.

Mom used reflective listening. This showed that Mom respected Carmen's feelings. It helped Mom see that Carmen thought Mom didn't have faith in her. This gave her a chance to show that she believed in Carmen and was willing to let her be responsible.

Mom gave Carmen a choice. Mom was friendly, but firm. Carmen agreed to the choice and accepted responsibility.

Mom helped Carmen explore alternatives. Carmen broke the agreement by telling her boss she would work late. Mom didn't say, "That's it! You promised not to work late. You're done with that job!" By listening carefully, she understood that Carmen didn't know how to handle the problem. She gave Carmen an opportunity to get back on track. She stayed respectful and helped Carmen think of ideas for keeping the job without working late. They brainstormed ideas and agreed to a plan. Carmen was able to stick to the agreement. She also learned a way to solve problems at work.

Mom followed through. When Carmen got a D on her geometry test, Mom listened again. She heard that Carmen had not studied enough. She heard that Carmen wanted to make excuses and get into a power struggle. So Mom had to follow through and have Carmen accept the consequence of her choice not to study. Doing that probably wasn't easy for Mom. She and Carmen had worked together to solve problems about work. That had been good for their relationship. It had helped them get along. Using consequences might stop those good feelings for a while. But what would Carmen learn if Mom gave in? She would see that she didn't have to live with the results of her choices. She would see that misbehaving let her be the boss. She wouldn't learn responsibility.

What Else Can Mom Do?

At other times, Mom still needs to find ways to encourage Carmen.

- She can notice effort and improvement in other areas.
- She can show that she appreciates Carmen.
- She can ask for Carmen's help.
- She can ask Carmen to join in making family decisions.
- She can encourage Carmen to go back to her job—or get another—once her grades improve.

All these things are ways that Mom can help Carmen learn to be both independent and responsible. And they are ways to keep building a good relationship.

If Mom doesn't give up, her relationship with Carmen won't be hurt by this experience. In the long run, it will improve. Over time, she may need to use consequences less. Carmen will have more respect for her. She'll know that Mom will expect her to accept the consequences of her choices. She may decide to make better choices.

Deciding What to Do

Whenever there is a problem with your teen, begin by deciding who owns the problem.

If Your Teen Owns the Problem

If your teen owns the problem, you have several options: You might decide to ignore it. You might listen for feelings and give feedback. You might offer to help your teen solve the problem.

Who Owns the Problem?

Ask yourself:

1. Are my rights being disrespected?

2. Could anybody get hurt?

3. Is someone's property threatened?

4. Is my teen unable to take this responsibility?

If you—or both of you—own the problem, decide what your teen's goal is. Respond in a way that your teen does not expect. Think about your purpose: to show that you understand and to help your teen be independent and responsible.

Use I-messages to tell how you feel. Work with your teenager to explore alternatives. If you need to, offer choices and let your teenager experience the consequences. Be firm, respectful, and encouraging.

Your teen may test you. Stay firm and respectful.

What Else Can I Do About Schoolwork?

The responsibility of schoolwork belongs to the teenager. Yet many parents believe the problem is partly theirs. After all, what teenagers learn in school affects the teens' future.

Remember, you can work together on problems that belong to your teen. You can help and influence your teen. Yet the problem still belongs to the teenager. You can't do the work for your teen. And you can't force your teen to study if the teen has decided not to.

Thinking About Schoolwork

At times, you may feel confused about how to handle the issue of schoolwork. If this happens, keep these two ideas in mind:

- Avoid power struggles.

- Look for ways to encourage.

School Is a Team Effort

Think of your teenager's learning as a team effort. The team members are the school, the teenager, and you:

- **The school's job is to teach.**

- **The teen's job is to learn.**

- **Your job is to set the stage— to provide opportunities for your teenager to succeed in school.**

Set the Stage for Success

Here are some things you can do to provide opportunities for success in school:

Encourage exercise. Exercise will help your teenager handle stress. It will help balance the mood swings that come with adolescence. It will help your teen's mind to be strong and alert.

Build your teenager's self-esteem. Give as much encouragement as possible. Encouraged teens want to learn.

Encourage responsibility at home. Responsibility at home will help build responsibility in school. It will also give your teen confidence. Many parents worry that if they leave an important job to the teen, the job won't be done. Expect that it will!

Many parents feel too busy to teach a teenager how to do some home jobs, like changing an air filter or ironing shirts. Take the time to work with your teen, rather than do these jobs by yourself.

Be involved with the school. Go to parent-teacher conferences. Attend sports, concerts, and plays. Most schools have an organization for parents and teachers. Join it. Volunteer to help with a school activity. Get involved in helping students raise money for events.

Join a parenting group. There might be a parenting group at your teen's school. There might be one at a church or the YMCA. Talking with other parents in a group helps. It is a good way to build your skills and your confidence. As you do, you will become a better parent. Working with your teenager will become easier. If you're reading this book on your own, consider joining a STEP/Teen parenting group.

Avoid rewards and punishment. Some parents punish teens for low grades. But punishment does not help young people learn to be responsible. Grounding a teenager or taking away TV or car privileges creates power struggles, not cooperation.

Some parents pay young people for good grades. But grades are not what is important. The learning is. If teenagers start to expect money for grades, they may focus on money, not on learning. They may lose the chance to enjoy the rewards of learning, hard work, and a job well done. These rewards come from inside the teen. Grades and money come from outside, from teachers and parents.

Be there for your teen. Some teens handle homework on their own without any trouble. They set their own schedules and get the job done without fuss. Others may need you to help them learn self-discipline:

- Give your teen limits and choices about when to get homework done.

- Make sure your teen has a place at home to do homework. Help your teenager find rides to the library. Offer your home as a study place for kids who are working on group projects.

- Be there to answer questions or review material with your teen at the end of a study period.

- Show an interest in the subjects your teen is studying. You might want to read a book your teen is reading. If your teen is studying politics, talk about politics at home. If your teen is studying astronomy, ask your teen to show you some constellations in the sky.

Let consequences happen at school. If your teen won't take responsibility, there will be consequences at school. Let your teenager experience those consequences. If you and the teacher or counselor feel you should help your teenager, use the skills you have learned in *Parenting Teenagers*. Set limits and offer choices. Explore alternatives.

Stay out of power struggles. If other ideas don't help, your teen may be seeking power or revenge. Calmly tell your teen, "I can't make you study. I'll leave it up to you. You can ask me for help." Be firm with yourself to stay out of power contests. With time, your teenager may decide to take responsibility.

Be encouraging. Many young people who do poorly in school are displaying inadequacy. Remember that a teen who shows helplessness is extremely discouraged. Notice and encourage every small step the teen makes—in schoolwork and in other areas. Focus on the teen's strengths. Say and show that you love your teen.

Use reflective listening. This skill will help you learn more about what's going on. Talk together about ways to get the needed help. Be sure to ask for the school's cooperation.

Teenagers who feel good about themselves are more likely to think for themselves.

What Can I Do About My Teen's Moods?

Chapter 1 and Chapter 2 talked about moodiness and why it happens.

Some Moodiness Is Normal

Some moodiness is normal. If your teen occasionally feels "down," be there to listen and encourage. Here are a few things parents sometimes hear from teens and some ways you might respond:

"I don't care." Some teens have an "I don't care" attitude. We call this *apathy*. Actually, these teens may care very much. But they don't believe they're in charge of their lives. They need a lot of encouragement. To help teens see that they *do* count, involve them in making decisions at home. Encourage them to choose classes and activities that might be of special interest. For teens who aren't interested in school activities, be creative.

Brendan doesn't feel he belongs at his school. He is happiest when he's painting and drawing. But he's taken all the art classes his school offers. Dad is worried about Brendan. He talks to the school counselor. The counselor knows about a special arts program at another school. She talks to Brendan about it. Brendan and the counselor figure out a way for Brendan to take art classes there for the last two hours of each school day. She helps him change his schedule and find a bus to the other school.

Sometimes "I don't care" and other types of apathy are a form of power. Check your feelings to see if this might be the case. If it is, avoid power struggles and let consequences occur.

"I'm bored." "There's never anything to do around here!" "School is so boring." What parent hasn't heard these words from a teenager? Many parents try to help bored young people by saying, "Why don't you do _____ ?"

That can be a mistake. Your teenager needs to be responsible for making life interesting. Often "I'm bored" is a bid for attention, or even power. Your best response probably is to ignore the remark.

"I can't . . . I'm scared . . . What if . . . ?" A young person's fear and worry tell us that the teen lacks self-confidence. Self-confidence doesn't grow overnight. But we can help our teens be more sure of themselves. How?

One way is to point out a time when they've handled something well. Another is to ask them to remember a time when they felt sure of themselves. When they feel scared or worried, suggest that they remember a good time. We can also help teens look for different ways to succeed.

Robin and a friend are having a snack. Dad comes into the kitchen. Aparna says, "Robin, you should try out for the chorus." Robin says, "I'd be scared in front of all those other kids." Megan says, "You sang with me in junior high chorus. I bet you'd make it." Robin says, "Yeah, but our high school chorus is three times bigger!"

Dad says nothing right then. Later, he talks to Robin about how she feels. He points out some times Robin did well, even when she wasn't sure she could. After that, Dad makes a point to keep encouraging Robin so that slowly, she will begin to feel more confident. If Robin tries and does not make it, Dad will know she'll feel discouraged. Then he can appreciate her efforts.

"I'm stressed." Stress is a response to pressure. If teens decide that life is too much for them, their bodies often find ways to prove them right. They may get stomach problems or headaches. They may get nervous tics.

Stress involves worrying and feeling unsure. If teens learn to deal with those feelings, then they should be able to avoid feeling too much stress. As with many things, your teen will notice the way you handle stress. Help your teen learn to relax. Chapter 1, page 20, has a "Just for You" activity called Ease the Stress. You might want to teach this activity to your teen.

Some Emotions May Be Danger Signals

Sometimes a teenager's moods and feelings get out of balance:

- It's one thing to feel sad. It's another to be depressed.

- It's one thing to be unhappy about your weight. It's another to hate your body.

- It's one thing to be angry about something. It's another to feel angry and violent much of the time.

- It's one thing to feel like you're in love. It's another to think about nothing else or not to see when a relationship is bad for you.

- It's one thing to want excitement and fun. It's another to drink and abuse other drugs.

In this chapter, we'll talk about three of these concerns: depression, body image, and anger and violence. In Chapter 7, we'll look more closely at alcohol and other drugs and at sex and dating.

Thinking About Confidence

Think of as many things as you can that your teen does well.

When your teen says "I can't," remember the things you've thought of. Remind your teen of all those things.

What About Depression?

Sadness and unhappiness are normal human emotions. A teenager who breaks up with a girlfriend or boyfriend often feels sad. The teen may need time to *mourn*—to "finish" the relationship by accepting that it's over. When we lose someone we care about, we feel sad. At times, this kind of sadness can be good.

Depression is different from sadness. Depression is a problem that usually won't go away by itself. It can involve both emotional and physical causes. Depressed teens quit growing emotionally and learning. Often, depressed teens will use alcohol or other drugs as a way to cope. This behavior can make depression continue or worsen.

Symptoms of Depression

- **a sad or "empty" mood that does not go away**

- **a loss of interest or pleasure in ordinary activities**

- **a loss of energy or a tired feeling that doesn't go away**

- **a definite change in school-work, sleeping, weight, or eating habits**

- **problems concentrating, remembering, or making decisions**

- **feeling very guilty, worth-less, or helpless**

- **talk of death or suicide, or suicide attempts**

- **crankiness that doesn't go away**

- **frequent crying**

- **aches and pains that don't go away with treatment**

What can you do?

The National Institutes of Health (NIH) say that if four or more symptoms last for more than two weeks, the teen should see a doctor or counselor. The teen may need medicine or counsel-ing. Often, both can be helpful.

Get Help

If you feel that your teen is depressed, get help right away. Call your doctor, school counselor, local mental health clinic, hospital emergency room, or a crisis hot line. (Look in the phone book under "Crisis Numbers" or "Suicide Prevention" or call the police emergency number.)

Stay Connected

Here are some other ways you can help a teen who is depressed:

Talk about suicide. If there's been a suicide in the news or at school, discuss it openly. This is a chance to hear what your teen is thinking. You can also help your teen understand what the person could have done instead.

Look for warning signals. Warning signals of suicide are listed at left. A teen who tries to commit suicide and fails may try again. A teen who talks about suicide may decide to commit suicide. It's not true that people who talk about suicide aren't likely to kill themselves. Most people who commit suicide do talk about it beforehand.

Listen. What you hear may be scary. But listening lets you know what's going on in your teen's mind. Use open questions to find out more.

Keep communication lines open. If you don't communicate well with your teen, find someone who does. That might be another person in your family. It might be an older brother or sister, or an aunt or uncle. It might be a stepparent. It might be a school counselor, a favorite teacher, or another adult the teen is close to. That person needs to give the teen a chance to discuss the troubled feelings.

Show love and give encouragement. A suicidal teen feels worthless and believes nothing will improve. The teen needs to feel worthwhile and loved. Look for ways to show that you love, accept, and value your teen.

What About Diets and Bad Eating Habits?

Every day our teens get messages from TV, movies, and magazines about the "perfect" body. At the same time, their bodies are changing. Both girls and boys can be self-conscious about how they look.

Many parents worry about teens who are overweight. Others worry about teens who always seem to be on diets, even though they look just fine to the parents. Many of us adults, too, have our own hang-ups about our looks, our weight, and food.

What if your teen says, "I'm fat! I hate the way I look!" You might ask, "What is your picture of how you'd like to look? How is your picture different from how you look now?" Remind your teenager that many different body shapes and sizes are normal.

Avoid a Focus on Weight and Food

Here are some other things you can do to prevent a focus on weight and food:

Don't make it a big deal. Make an effort not to focus on looks and food. Don't interfere with your teen's eating. Don't suggest diets. Don't say, "An apple would be better for you than that candy bar" or "I have a coupon for a diet program. Would you like to try it?" If your teen asks for help with a diet and you feel it would be helpful, *do* support your teen. But don't be the one to keep bringing up the subject.

Look at what you say and do. Do you say, "Clean your plate"? That encourages teens to eat even if they're full. Do you say, "No snacks! You'll spoil your dinner?" Do you eat healthy foods yourself? Do you criticize the way *you* look? Your teenager may be influenced by what you do and say.

Most teens who commit suicide talk about it beforehand.

Three Common Eating Disorders

- **Obesity.** In most cases, a teen who is <u>obese</u>—very overweight—is eating out of control. Food has become an addiction.

- **Anorexia.** This disorder usually occurs in girls. The teen believes that she is fat, even though she's thin. She starves herself to avoid being "fat" at all costs.

- **Bulimia.** This is also more common with girls than boys. As with anorexia, the teen feels fat, even if she's thin. But the teen <u>binges</u>—eats far too much—and then makes herself throw up so she won't gain weight. With both anorexia and bulimia, teens often use <u>laxatives</u> or take <u>diuretics</u> (often in diet pills).

Enjoy lots of different foods. Keep lots of healthy food on hand. Arrange for the whole family to eat together every day, or several times a week. And don't completely get rid of your teen's favorite foods. If your teen likes chocolate cookies, having some in the cupboard is okay.

Talk about media images. Discuss how the "perfect" bodies in magazines and on TV don't look like most people. Share with your teen what you've learned from TV shows or magazine articles about what a normal body really is. Share your own stories about how you felt about your body when you were a teen.

Be encouraging. A teen who is overly worried about looks needs a boost in confidence. Use the encouragement skills you have learned to help your teen feel loved, accepted, and worthwhile. Focus on your teen's strengths: "You have a beautiful smile." "The aerobics class seems to be making you stronger."

An Eating Disorder Is Different

Some teens do have *eating disorders*. There are three common eating disorders: *obesity*, *anorexia*, and *bulimia*.

Gina's mother, Linda, is worried about 18-year-old Gina. Gina looks very thin, though she doesn't seem to know it. She is critical of how she looks. On the phone, she says to her friend, "I can't even let Zach <u>see</u> me till I lose five more pounds!" She stands in front of the mirror and says, "Look at that ugly fat on my arms."

Linda has noticed that Gina eats quite a bit at meals. It doesn't make sense that Gina is losing weight. One night after supper, Linda goes past the bathroom and hears Gina throwing up. The next night, Gina again eats a big dinner. After she leaves the table, her brother Raoul says, "I bet she's going to stick her finger down her throat." Linda asks Raoul, "Why do you say that?" Raoul says, "That's what she does after lunch at school. Lynn's sister saw her."

Bulimia is serious. What can Linda do to help Gina?

Use I-messages and reflective listening. Linda can say to Gina, "When I see how thin you're getting, I worry that you might be sick." If Gina denies being too thin, Linda might say, "I heard you throwing up, Gina. When you throw up for no reason, I feel really scared. It seems like you're making yourself do it, and that's not good for your body." Gina might get angry and say, "You have no right to hang out by the bathroom door listening to me! Can't I have any privacy?" Then Linda might answer, "You're angry with me because you feel like I'm snooping. I really did just happen to hear you, Gina. But I'm very worried. Why do you feel you need to be thinner?"

Explore alternatives. This is a difficult balance. Linda needs to listen to Gina's feelings. She needs to let Gina be in charge of herself as much as possible. Staying respectful, Linda can ask what steps Gina will take to stop losing so much weight and throwing up.

Get professional help. Linda needs to keep a close eye on Gina and talk to her about how things are going. If she sees that Gina is still too thin or acting strangely, the problem belongs to Linda. Gina's health and safety are in danger. Linda will need to get help for Gina. She can talk to a doctor. She can look for a clinic for eating disorders or look for a counselor. Someone at Gina's school might be able to help Linda find these people.

A teen with an eating disorder is discouraged. The teen feels unable to control her body. Her body becomes her enemy.

An obese teen may have initally used food as a substitute for companionship or just something to do when she wanted more attention. Eventually, she may become addicted to food or eating. She begins to feel that food controls her rather than that she has control over what and how much she eats.

A teen with anorexia or bulimia may see a parent or others as being in control of her every move. She feels discouraged. She may believe the only thing she can control is her body. She may refuse to eat. Or, she may try to control her body weight by bingeing and throwing up. Her eating behaviors may also become addictive. Then, she may feel she cannot even control her body.

With any eating disorder, a teen needs help from a physician or other health professional. Teens with eating disorders also need all of the love and encouragement a parent can give.

What About Anger and Violence?

Violence is all around us. We see it on TV. We read about it in the newspaper. Some people live with violence in their homes. Parents worry about violence. The most important thing you can do about violence is to teach your teen *nonviolence.*

Remember, you also are a model for your teen. Hitting is a form of violence. If you hit others, teens may see hitting as acceptable adult behavior. We can think of no reason for one person to hit another. Yelling also doesn't help. Few people want to cooperate after being yelled at.

Hitting and yelling won't solve problems. They make problems worse. Page 52 in Chapter 3 has more ideas about what to do when you feel like hitting or yelling.

Help Your Teen Deal With Anger

Just as they can be sad or excited, teens can sometimes become very angry. If the anger is toward you, don't get involved in power or revenge contests. Tantrums need an audience—so don't be your teen's audience! If the anger doesn't involve you, you might:

- Use reflective listening to let your teen know what you hear: "You're very angry with Rico. Want to talk about it?"

- Point out how the anger gets in the way of solving problems:"I wonder what you could do to feel better about this?"

- Later, when your teen is calmer, talk about ways to deal with anger. Some teens find that exercise helps them deal with anger *and* avoid getting so angry to begin with. Other teens might like to listen to music, call a friend, write in a journal, or draw. Point out to your teen that anger gets in the way of solving problems. Help your teen see that being able to solve problems with someone lets both people feel in control. Then no one needs to be angry.

A teen who is angry much of the time needs professional help. This is true whether the anger involves parents or not.

Discourage Violent TV, Movies, Comics, Computer Games, and Music

Having rules about violent materials in your home is okay. You have the right to expect your teenager to respect your wish for no violent TV, comics, music, or games.

We all know this issue isn't easy or simple. A 16 year old can easily get into an R-rated movie. A 14 year old can find violence on the television. A 12 year old can hide a comic book. And all teens spend time in other homes, where the rules are often different.

With teens, talking about why you are setting those limits is important. Watch some programs yourself to decide on your limits. Watch TV *with* your teen too. This is a good way to deal with this kind of violence.

Different people have different feelings about what "violence" means and how much they will accept. One parent is comfortable with westerns or fantasy movies. Another parent thinks football games are too violent. Think about your own ideas on violence. Take the time to explain your feelings to your teen. Listen to your teen's feelings too. Explore alternatives about what programs are and aren't okay.

Parents sometimes send teens unintended messages about violence.

Teenagers Worry About Violence

You may find that your teen wants to talk to you. Young people worry about violence too:

B. J. is 14. Now that he's in ninth grade, he goes to the local high school. Some boys from a gang want B. J. to be in their gang. One of the boys warns him not to hang out with Carrie, a girl B. J. met in his English class. B. J. tells the boy, "I don't want to be in any gang. I don't want to hurt anybody. Leave me alone." B. J. is scared. He tells his parents about what has happened. "I know they won't leave me alone," B. J. says. "What can I do?"

This is a big problem. Gangs don't respect people's rights. Someone might get hurt. B. J. can't figure this out alone.

What Can Mom and Dad Do?

B. J.'s parents need to listen to his feelings. He needs to know they are there for him. And that is not enough. B. J.'s parents can't make the world completely safe. But they can help B. J. avoid gangs:

- They can tell B. J. he did the right thing. Saying no to the boys showed courage. It shows he knows what's right.

- They can talk about what B. J. could do next time. They can ask for his ideas. He may have some good ones and some not so good ones. His parents need to hear those so they can help him do the safest thing. As they talk, they can give B. J. their ideas too.

Encouragement
STEP

Notice when your teen does helpful things. Notice when he or she is responsible. Give friendly I-messages or say "I noticed." Here are some examples:

- **"I noticed that you gave the dog a bath. She smells <u>much</u> better!"**

- **"I noticed that you made the juice this morning. Thanks."**

- They can help B. J. figure out how to get to know kids in the new school who aren't involved with gangs. B. J. might want to try out for a sport. He may want to work on the yearbook or newspaper.

- They also need to contact the school and find out more about gangs in B. J.'s school. What is it doing to deal with the problem? What does the school suggest to help B. J. stay safe and enjoy his new school?

B. J.'s parents can also look for other ways to help keep B. J. safe:

- There may be an after-school program at a community center.

- A church, synagogue, or mosque may be open as a safe place for kids to study and hang out.

- There may be programs through the police department.

- There may be groups of parents working to keep their teenagers safe. B. J.'s parents could join a group like that. They could even start one.

Helping Teens Avoid Gangs

Gangs are a serious problem. No one can make gangs simply go away. As parents, we can help our teenagers avoid getting involved in gangs. How?

Help them feel loved. When you encourage your teen, you help your teen feel loved. When you accept your teen, you help your teen feel wanted. We all need to know that we are loved. Teenagers need to feel this love too. Then they will be less likely to look for "love" in a gang.

Help them feel powerful. Teenagers need to feel powerful. One way to give young people power is to keep limits reasonable and offer choices. Provide lots of ways for teens to make decisions. They will be less likely to want to join a gang to get power.

Help them feel needed. We can help our teens know that they are important to us. We show this when we expect them to cooperate. We show this when we give them responsibilities and ask for their ideas and help. We can tell our teens, too, how much their help means to us. We can help our teenagers feel like important members of our family. Then they will be less likely to seek out the "family" of a gang.

You Have Taken Another Big Step

In Chapter 6, you have learned that you can use your parenting skills and approaches in many ways:

- You have learned what questions to ask yourself so that you can decide what to do.
- You have seen ways you can use your skills to help your teen deal with everyday problems.
- You have thought about ways to help your teen avoid and deal with serious problems.
- You have remembered the importance of encouragement.

THIS WEEK

When problems arise, think about what to do *before* you act. Decide who owns the problem. Think about your purpose. Decide how you can best help. Ask yourself:

- What is my teen's goal?
- Can I listen for feelings?
- Can I use an I-message?
- Can we explore alternatives?
- Can I give a choice?
- How can I encourage my teen?

Plan a way to begin to solve the problem with your teenager.

For Your *Family*

Continue with family meetings. When you meet, remind people of the purpose of family meetings:

- to share good feelings
- to have fun together
- to make plans
- to talk about problems and help each other

Ask your family, "How does anyone feel about our meetings? How are they helping us?" If your family is having trouble working together, talk about this. Listen to feelings. Share your own feelings too. Ask for ideas on how to work together better. Make agreements.

JUST FOR YOU

What's Your Priority?

We all need to belong. How we do this depends on our *priorities*—those things that are most important to us. One set of priorities has to do with how we relate to other people.

To find your own priorities, take this simple test. Think about each of the following ideas. Which is most important to you? Put a "1" next to it. Put a "2" by the next most important idea. Rank the others "3" and "4."

_____ **A.** I want to avoid being rejected.

_____ **B.** I want to avoid being embarrassed.

_____ **C.** I want to avoid stress or conflict.

_____ **D.** I want to avoid being unproductive.

A. If you ranked this choice first, *pleasing* is probably your highest priority. You want to be liked by other people.

B. If you ranked this choice first, *control* is probably your highest priority. You want to be in charge. You don't want to be controlled by someone else.

C. If you ranked this choice first, *comfort* is probably your highest priority. You don't want to be disturbed by stress or conflict.

D. If you ranked this choice first, *excellence* is probably your highest priority. You want to have meaning in your life.

The following chart lists some of the ways the different priorities can affect you and your teenager.

Priority	Pluses for you	Minuses for you	Pluses for your teen	Minuses for your teen
Pleasing	You may get along with others. You may know what people want.	You may feel (and be) taken advantage of, disrespected.	May experience less conflict, may feel easily understood.	May be disrespectful, take advantage of others.
Control	You may be logical and organized.	You may find it hard to get close to people to share feelings.	May learn limits and organization.	May face power contests, be afraid to share feelings.
Comfort	You may be easygoing and have few conflicts.	You may feel unfulfilled, a lack of accomplishment.	May experience less conflict, feel able to pursue own interests.	Interests may go unrecognized, seem unimportant.
Excellence	You may be very capable and creative.	You may feel overburdened, overresponsible.	May be creative, have positive outlook on life.	May feel inadequate, need to be perfect.

- What positive effects does your priority have on your life? on your approach to parenting?
- What negative effects does it have?
- What changes might you want to make?

POINTS TO REMEMBER

1. The approach you use with your teen depends on what is happening.

2. To decide what to do, ask yourself who owns the problem, what the teen's goal is, what your purpose is, and how you can best help.

3. With schoolwork, your job is to help your teen be ready and able to succeed. Do this by:
   - encouraging your teen to be healthy and responsible
   - getting involved with school and other parents
   - avoiding rewards and punishment
   - being there for your teen
   - letting consequences happen
   - using encouragement

4. Some moodiness is normal. Use reflective listening and I-messages to help your teen. Don't get involved if your teen wants attention or a power struggle.

5. Depression is different from sadness. It can involve both emotional and physical causes.

6. To help your teen have a healthy body image:
   - Don't focus on weight and food.
   - Provide lots of healthy foods, as well as a few special snacks.
   - Talk about "perfect" bodies in the media.
   - Be encouraging.

7. If your teen is depressed or has an eating disorder, get help. Keep communicating with your teen. Give love and encouragement.

8. To encourage nonviolence, decide not to hit and to set and talk about limits on violent TV, movies, comics, computer games, and music.

9. To help your teen deal with anger:
   - Use reflective listening and I-messages.
   - Help your teen find a way to solve the problem.
   - Talk about ways to avoid and get rid of anger.

10. To help your teenager avoid gangs, encourage the teen to get involved in safe activities. Work to help your teen feel loved, powerful, and needed.

11. You can't guarantee your teen's safety. But you can use your parenting skills to help your teenager avoid serious problems and make good choices.

Chart 6

EFFECTIVE APPROACHES TO PROBLEMS

Approach	Who owns the problem?	What's your purpose?	What can you say?
Reflective listening	Teen	To show you understand teen's problem	"You sound very worried about the test." "You're hurt that Teri's going to the dance with Dave?"
I-message	Parent	To say respectfully how teen's behavior affects you	"When you pierce your nose and eyebrows, I feel worried because you could get an infection." "When you borrow tools and don't return them, I feel frustrated because I don't have them when I need them."
Exploring alternatives	Teen	To help teen decide how to solve problem	"What are some ways you could solve this problem?" "Which idea do you like best?" "Are you willing to do this until _____?"
	Parent/ Parent and teen	To work out agreements with teen	"What can we do to work out this problem we have?" "Do we both agree on this idea?" "What will we do if one of us breaks the agreement?"
Consequences	Teen	To allow teen to make and live with choices	Teen who forgets coat on cold day gets cold. Teen who skips practice doesn't get to play in the game (rules set by coach, not involving parent).
	Parent/ Parent and teen	To set or work with teen to set choices and consequences for problem behavior	Teen who quickly spends allowance does not receive more money until next allowance day. Teen who comes home after curfew does not go out next night.

CHAPTER SEVEN

Deciding What to Do: Part 2

In Chapter 6, you looked at a way to decide how to handle challenges with your teenager. In this chapter, you'll keep thinking about ways to deal with other common challenges involving your teenager.

Six Skills for Helping Your Teen

- **Identifying the goal** helps you decide how to respond.
- **Reflective listening** is helpful when your teen owns the problem.
- **I-messages** help you tell how you feel when you own the problem.
- **Exploring alternatives** is helpful no matter who owns the problem.
- **Giving choices** and opportunities to make decisions depends on who owns the problem.
- **Encouragement** is the cornerstone of your relationship with your teen. Use it as often as you can.

Here's what you will learn . . .

- Sisters and brothers can be expected to get along and solve their own problems.
- You can work to build trust with your teen and use your skills if lying or stealing becomes a problem.
- Talking with your teen about the choices and consequences of sex is important.
- Your skills can be used to help your teen avoid being involved with drugs.
- You can practice and use all your parenting skills to keep working on your relationship with your teen.

What About When Sisters and Brothers Argue?

Brothers and sisters often fight or quarrel. Fighting doesn't always go away as children grow to be teens. In fact, fighting can be so common that many parents believe it is "normal." The parents *expect* sisters and brothers to fight.

Jamal is 15 and Maurice is 12. They are brothers. Maurice likes to hang out with Jamal and his friends. He follows them into the living room to watch TV with them. He tags along to the rec center to play basketball.

Jamal wants to be alone with his friends. He gets mad at Maurice and says, "Leave us alone! Go find some <u>little</u> kids to play with!" Soon Jamal and Maurice are in a fight.

Often, the boys try to get Dad involved in their fight. Maurice says, "Jamal's mean to me. He won't let me watch TV in my own living room!" Or Jamal says, "Make him leave me and my friends alone."

What Can Dad Do?

Jamal and Maurice own the problem of getting along with each other. Trying to stop the fighting can make it worse. No matter what Dad does, one of the boys will probably feel that Dad is taking sides with the other.

When teenagers and younger children fight, they often have a goal. It might be to get the parent's attention. Maybe they want to show the parent they can do what they want, to demonstrate power. One young person might pick on another who seems to be the parent's "favorite," with a goal of revenge against the parent.

Dad can stay out of the conflict. Dad can't make Jamal and Maurice get along better. But he can refuse to get involved. When he starts doing this, Maurice and Jamal's fights may get worse before they get better. The boys may try to pull Dad back into the struggle by tattling. Dad can say: "This problem is for you and your brother to solve. I know you'll figure it out." This shows the boys that Dad believes they can get along.

Dad can use a consequence. If there is hitting, biting, or kicking, the problem will become Dad's as well. Then he can use a consequence. He can say: "One of you might get hurt. You can handle your problem without hitting, or you each can have some time-out alone." If the hitting continues, Dad will need to follow through. If Jamal's friends are over, he'll need to send them home and separate the two boys.

Deciding What to Do

Decide who owns the problem. Think about your purpose. Decide how you can best help. Ask yourself:

- What is my teen's goal?
- Can I listen for feelings? Can I use an I-message?
- Can we talk it through?
- Can I give a choice?
- How can I encourage my teen?

Dad can help each boy explore alternatives. If Maurice never leaves Jamal alone, that isn't fair to Jamal. Dad might use reflective listening to find out why Maurice doesn't spend time with friends of his own. He could help Maurice think of other things to do. He might be able to help him find ways to be more respectful. Then maybe Jamal will want to spend more time with Maurice.

Dad can encourage Jamal to be respectful too. Jamal may want some help figuring out ways to deal with Maurice.

What About Lying and Stealing?

Sometimes a teenager will lie. Sometimes a teen takes something that does not belong to him or her. That does not mean the teen will grow up to be a liar or thief.

Adults Lie Too

Most parents see lies as a sign their teen doesn't trust them. Yet many parents lie too:

- The phone might ring when a parent doesn't want to talk. The parent might say to the teen, "Tell her I'm not home."

- To save money at the movies, a parent may pretend a 13 year old is younger, to pay for a child-priced ticket.

These may seem like small things. But what do young people learn when parents are not honest? That lying is sometimes okay.

Thinking About Arguments Between Brothers and Sisters

Think about when your kids argue. Ask yourself:

- **What do I usually do when my kids fight? Does it help?**

- **What else can I do?**

Decide what you will do the next time there's fighting. Stick to your plan.

Teens are only too aware of the "little white lies" adults tell.

Lying Has a Goal

Teens may lie to gain the attention of parents or peers. They may lie to escape punishment or seek revenge. Sometimes teens lie to impress their friends.

Chloe is 16. Her family has moved from California to Wisconsin. Chloe likes to skateboard. She wants to make friends with a group who does a lot of skateboarding. Chloe's mom hears Chloe on the phone talking to a new friend. Chloe says that back in California she hung out with a famous skateboard champion. She says she did skateboard stunts in music videos. Mom knows that Chloe's stories aren't true.

What Can Mom Do?

Mom is probably bothered to hear Chloe lying. Still, Chloe owns the problem of telling lies to her new friends.

Exploring alternatives can help teens "think out loud."

Mom might decide to ignore it. Over time, Chloe will probably feel more at home with her new friends. Then she might not feel like she needs to lie to be accepted. On the other hand, the friends may not believe Chloe. The consequence of having friends catch her lying may help her make a better choice in the future.

Mom can give positive attention. Chloe's lies tell Mom that Chloe feels unsure of herself. Without talking about the lies, Mom can find ways to give Chloe positive attention. She can point out strengths that make Chloe a good friend. Mom might say, "Thanks for returning my library books. I appreciate how I can count on you." Or she might say, "You have a way of looking on the bright side. That helps me when I'm feeling down. I'm sure your friends appreciate that about you too."

Mom can use reflective listening and I-messages. Mom might decide to give Chloe a chance to talk about her feelings. She could tell her daughter, "I overheard you on the phone today. It sounds like you really want to impress your new friends." If Chloe is willing to talk, Mom will have a chance to help her think about the possible consequences of lying: "When I hear you telling stories, I feel concerned that your friends will figure out they're not true. Have you thought about what might happen then?"

Mom can help Chloe explore alternatives. Exploring alternatives can help Chloe "think out loud." It can help her see that there are probably ways to make friends without lying. It can show her that Mom believes she is capable of making friends.

Lying Is Tied to Trust

If your teen lies to you, your rights are disrespected. Then you own the problem. For a one-time lie, you may decide to ignore the problem. But if you do that too often, you're likely to send your teen the message that lying has a payoff—that it works.

Kyle is 14. On Friday nights, he often wants to stay over at his friend Joe's home. One Saturday morning Kyle comes home smelling like beer. His dad says, "I smell beer. Were you and Joe drinking last night?" "No," says Kyle. "We don't drink. But his dad had friends over, and they were drinking. That's probably what you smell." "Oh," says Dad.

The next week, Kyle comes home tired and cranky. His eyes are bloodshot. His mom says, "Kyle, you look hungover. Are you sure you and Joe weren't drinking?" Kyle says, "Mom! I told you we don't drink!" Mom says, "But you keep coming home so tired." Kyle says, "I work hard all week. And I don't get much sleep. Of course I'm tired on Saturday." Mom says, "Maybe you and Joe should sleep here." Kyle says, "Don't you trust me?" Mom says, "Of course I do, but—" Kyle interrupts, "Joe's got great cable stations. And he lives right by the school, so we can walk to games. I like staying there!" Mom sighs. "Okay, okay" she says. "You'd better take a nap."

What Can Mom and Dad Do?

In their hearts, Kyle's parents know that their son is drinking. But they don't want to face it. Instead, they accept his lies. What does that tell Kyle? It tells him that lying works for him. That encourages a habit of lying. It may also send the message that his parents don't really care about him. It also leaves Kyle free to drink. Kyle's parents need to deal with their son's lying *and* drinking.

Use I-messages and reflective listening. Kyle's parents can say to Kyle, "When we're lied to, we feel worried, because we know you're doing something you feel is wrong." Kyle may say, "I don't see why you don't trust me!" They might answer, "You feel we're unfair not to trust you. But when you're dishonest, we feel unfairly treated too. We want to trust you, but we can't." Kyle's parents can remain calm. They may begin to learn more about what's happening on Friday nights.

Provide or negotiate consequences. Kyle needs to experience the consequences of lying. His parents might say, "Since you've decided to lie to us, you'll need to stay home this Friday night. Next week you can have another chance to tell us the truth about what you plan to do." They might also ask their son, "We can't accept lying. What will you do to earn back our trust?"

Offer choices. For future Friday nights, Kyle's parents could offer several choices:

- "You may stay at Joe's as long as his dad assures us there won't be any drinking. Otherwise, you and Joe can sleep here."

- "We can drive you to the game and pick you up. We'll be glad to give Joe a ride too. Or you can find something to do at home. It's up to you."

- "You can have your friends here after the game as long as there's no drinking."

- "You can go to the party after the game as long as you agree to call if anyone's drinking. We agree to pick you up without asking questions."

Set the Stage for the Truth

Teenagers need freedom and trust. Trust is a difficult issue. You can't stop your teen from ever lying. But by following these guidelines, you can help make it easier for your teen to tell the truth:

Keep limits reasonable. Don't set up unrealistic expectations. Saying no to everything is unrealistic: "You can't go to that movie." "No, you can't ride with Toban." "You can't play those albums in this home!" "I don't want to see you hanging out with Dana!" When the only thing teens hear is "You *can't,*" they may feel that they have no choice but to lie.

Don't play detective. "Where did you go?" "Who were you with?" "What did you do?" "Why did you do that?" Too many closed questions may invite a teen to lie.

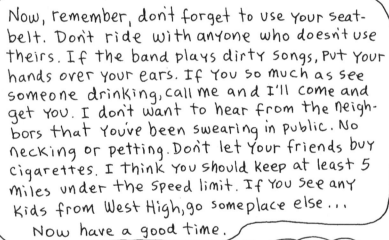

It's not realistic to say no to everything.

Make telling the truth safe. When parents punish or put teens down, they make telling the truth dangerous for teens. How do you make being honest with you safe for your teen? By being respectful. By using consequences rather than punishment.

Desiree, 17, enters the room, obviously sad. She tells her stepmom, Sharee, "I skipped school Friday. The coach found out and told me I couldn't play this week. I can't believe I did that!" Sharee says, "Not playing is really disappointing to you."

Sharee doesn't say, "How dare you?" or "You've really let me down!" She knows that Desiree already feels bad. And she doesn't say, "You're grounded!" The coach has already given Desiree a consequence for her misbehavior. Because her stepmom stays respectful, Desiree knows it's safe to tell the truth—even when she's done something wrong.

Expect your teen to be honest. Don't set things up to try to catch your teenager in a lie. That tells your teen that you *expect* lying. It says that you don't believe your teenager can be trusted.

Show that you appreciate the truth. "I'm not willing to accept what you did, and we'll need to discuss what to do about it. But I know it took real courage for you to tell me this, and I'm glad you told me."

Lying is a sign of a problem in your relationship. If your teen is lying to you, work to open up lines of communication.

My Teen Lied to Me—What Can I Do?

1. Don't panic! Telling a lie or two doesn't make your teen a bad person. It doesn't mean your teen will begin to lie all the time. It also does not mean you'll never be able to trust your teen again. Remember to "separate the deed from the doer."

2. Use an I-message. "When you don't tell me the truth, I feel really disappointed because I've always been able to depend on what you say to me." This tells your teen how you feel. It shows that you still respect your teen.

3. Deal with what has happened. Don't accuse. Just deal with the specific situation. If necessary, use logical consequences: "I know you had your friends in while we were gone, because I smell smoke. So the next time we go out, you'll have to go with us or go to your aunt's."

Stealing Has a Goal Too

Sometimes teens steal for excitement or to impress their friends. Stealing can also involve attention, power, or revenge.

The more accepting, encouraging, and trusting your relationship, the less likely that your teen will feel the need to lie.

Lupe is 15. She goes shopping with her friend Morgan. She tries on a shirt and pair of pants. Morgan says, "Lupe, you look <u>so</u> great in that outfit! You should get it!" Lupe sees that the two items together cost about $60. Lupe says, "I can't afford it." Morgan says, "Would your mom buy it for you?" Lupe says, "No way—I get a monthly allowance for clothes." Morgan says, "Maybe she'd give you next month's allowance early." Lupe says, "No. She'd never do it." Morgan says, "Lupe, that outfit is just perfect for you." Lupe says no more. But she can't stop thinking about the outfit.

That night, Lupe sees her mom's purse on the counter. Mom is in the bathroom. Looking in Mom's wallet, Lupe sees a bunch of $20 bills. Quickly, she takes $60.

The next day, Lupe goes back to the store after school. She buys the outfit. That night, Mom comes into Lupe's room to say goodnight. This morning she saw that $60 was gone from her wallet. Now she sees Lupe's new outfit. She looks at the price tags. Mom feels shocked and hurt. She says to Lupe, "I see you bought a new outfit." Lupe says, "What's that supposed to mean?" Mom says, "Why should it mean anything?" Lupe says, "You used that 'snooping voice' I hate." Mom asks, "Lupe, did you take money from my purse to pay for this outfit?" Glaring, Lupe says, "How else was I gonna buy it? It'd take me months to save the money with that stupid allowance you give me! No one else has to buy their own clothes!"

What Can Mom Do?

Mom feels hurt. She wants to say, "How dare you steal from me!" She wonders, "How did my own daughter turn out so spoiled?" She thinks about telling Lupe, "That's it! You're grounded!"

But Mom doesn't want to join Lupe in a battle of revenge. She thinks about her purpose: to help Lupe take responsibility for her mistake and to encourage Lupe not to steal again.

Mom states her feelings by using an I-message: "When you steal from me, I feel hurt and disappointed. I want to trust you, but it seems like I can't." Lupe says, "I hate always having to save my money and choose what to buy and what not to buy. All my friends have more money than I do." Mom uses reflective listening: "Sounds like you're really angry because your friends buy more clothes than you do." Lupe stares angrily at her mother. She says rudely, "Duh!"

Mom stays respectful: "How will you pay me back the sixty dollars?" Lupe says, "It'll take forever to do that on my allowance!" Mom says, "You get enough allowance to pay me back in less than two months." Lupe says, "But then I won't have any money!" Mom says, "Is there some way you can earn some extra money?" Glaring, Lupe says, "I suppose so. But it means I'll have to babysit—which I hate!"

Mom sees that Lupe still wants a battle. Mom remains calm and respectful: "Why don't you think about it tonight. Tomorrow night you can tell me your plan for paying me back. I know you'll figure it out."

When a Teen Shoplifts

If you believe that your teen has stolen something from a store, ask where the item came from. Have your teen experience the consequence of stealing. You might say, "You need to return this. Do you want me to go with you?" If the police get involved, don't panic. A brush with the police can have a big effect on many teens. Chapter 5, pages 100–101, also discuss shoplifting.

What About Sex?

Some parents deal with the issue of sex by *not* dealing with it. They avoid talking about sex and hope that their teen will stay safe.

Other parents try to forbid their teen to be sexual. They tell their teen only that sex is wrong and that the teen must wait. They don't help their teen see that sexual feelings are normal and natural. They don't help their teen feel good about their changing body.

Neither of these approaches will help teens make good choices about sex. Sex is a fact of life. We can't tell teens not to think about sex. We can't force them not to feel sexual urges. We can't turn off their hormones. And we can't erase the pressure that comes from TV, magazines, music, and advertisers. What can we do to help our teens make responsible choices?

Talk About It

What you tell your teen about your views on sex depends on your values. That will be different for each parent. As always:

- Listen to your teen's words, face, and body language.
- Ask open questions.
- State your own feelings respectfully.
- Show faith in your teen's ability to make good decisions.

When you talk about sex, you are talking about choices. Perhaps the most important message to give your teen is that there really *are* choices to be made! It's true that everyone is sexual. That doesn't mean that everyone has to have sex.

Talking About Choices

Teenagers have sex for a number of reasons. Some may long for the closeness and love that can go with sex. Some may want pleasure or excitement. Some may feel pressured by a boyfriend or

A Word About Repeated Lying or Stealing

If your teen lies or steals again and again, the problem is serious. Get help for your teenager. Talk to the principal, counselor, or social worker at your teen's school.

girlfriend. They may fear losing the person if they don't give in to having sex. Some teens use sex as a way to get attention, power, or revenge. Some teenagers have sex with the goal of having a baby. Those teens are extremely discouraged. They feel such a need for love that having a baby of their own seems the only way to get it. Or they may believe that having a baby will help them get out of the house and be on their own.

All of these reasons have something in common. They are a way for the teens to belong. Talking together will help you learn about why your teen may want to have sex. It will help you learn how sex might help your teen belong. If you know that, you can help your teen find other ways to belong. You will be able to help your teen make a responsible choice.

Tai is 16. Lately it seems that all his friends talk about is sex. Tai has a girlfriend named Fran. Tai's friends keep teasing him about her: "Wow! That Fran is really hot! When are you gonna do it with her?"

Tai's dad has overheard Tai's friends tease in that way. He guesses that Tai may be thinking about having sex with Fran. He decides to talk about this with Tai.

Dad begins carefully. He says to Tai, "Your friends are giving you a pretty rough time about Fran." Tai is embarrassed. He says, "They're just stupid. I wish they'd get off my case." Dad says, "You sound kind of disgusted with them." Tai says, "Fran and I don't want to do it. The guys would laugh me out of school if they knew how I feel."

Dad now knows that Tai has made a choice not to have sex with Fran. He wants to let his son know he thinks it's a wise choice. But he doesn't want to close the door to further talking. Dad says, "It must be nice to have a girlfriend who feels the same way you do about waiting to have sex." Tai doesn't look like he agrees. He pauses, then says, "She wants to stay a virgin till she gets married." Dad says, "And you respect that." "Yeah . . . I guess," says Tai.

Things feel awkward. Dad can tell that Tai isn't completely sure. Dad thinks for a minute. Then he says, "Tai, I'm glad that you respect Fran's feelings. I know that can't be easy for you." Tai looks embarrassed. "Yeah," he mumbles. Dad says, "There are things that make handling your feelings easier. Working out. Shooting hoops. You know." Tai says, "Yeah, I know." Dad says, "If the guys—or Fran—get on your nerves, I'd be glad to talk some more." Tai says, "Thanks." Dad grins and says, "Want to shoot a few baskets with me?"

A lot has happened in this conversation. Dad has learned that Tai is not sure about having sex. That is true for many teenagers. With all the talk of sex, assuming that all teens want to have it is easy. That's not always the case—for girls *or* boys. Dad has had a chance to show that Tai can talk safely about sex and his feelings for Fran. He's let his son know that there's nothing wrong with sexual feelings. He's suggested ways to deal with those feelings too.

Most important, Dad has opened the door for more conversations about sex. He's only opened the door a little. He'll want to keep opening it a bit at a time in the weeks and months to come.

What Else Can Dad Do?

Dad can talk with Tai not only at times of crisis, but also at other times. Dad wants to be sure his son knows the consequences of sexual behavior. He also wants to listen to Tai. Here some things they could discuss.

The consequences of sexual behavior. Dad can talk to Tai about the chance of getting AIDS (acquired immune deficiency syndrome) or other STDs (sexually transmitted diseases) like herpes, syphilis, chlamydia, or gonorrhea. He can talk about how easy it can be for a young woman to get pregnant—even if a couple is using a condom or other form of birth control. He can talk about how pregnancy changes the life of the girl, the boy, and their families. It brings up big questions about adoption, abortion, and early marriage. What could that mean for teenagers' future plans? What could it mean for the baby?

Abstinence. Dad can also talk with Tai about staying with his choice not to have sexual intercourse. This is called *abstinence*. What are the consequences of abstinence? There is no risk of pregnancy. There is little risk of disease. For some teens, good feelings go with abstinence. They may help a teen's self-esteem. And many teens are not emotionally ready to have sex. Waiting gives them time to grow up some more. Waiting to be older and to have a stronger relationship is a sign of real responsibility.

Drinking, drugs, and sex. Dad should talk to Tai about the connection between drinking, drugs, and sex. Many teens lose their willpower if they have even a small amount to drink. That is true with illegal drugs like marijuana or pills too.

Date rape. Dad needs to talk to Tai about date rape. Both girls and boys need to understand that forcing someone to have sex is rape. A teen who is forced into sex needs to know a parent or other adult will be there to help.

Responsible sex. Dad also needs to talk with Tai about responsible sex. Responsible sex means doing what both people want to do. It means being safe: using condoms, using reliable birth control, and seeing a doctor regularly.

Assuming that all teens want to have sex is easy. That's not always the case—for girls or boys.

Some parents don't want to talk about responsible sex. They may believe their teens should not use any sexual behaviors, including masturbation—period. Their religious faith may say that condoms or birth control pills are wrong. It's up to you to decide what to talk about with your teen.

But some teenagers will decide to have sex no matter what parents say. You might choose not to teach your teenager about these things. In any case, you need to think ahead about how you will handle the consequences if your teen does have sex.

Teen pregnancy. Teen pregnancies occur for many reasons, including these:

- lack of information
- a need for love and acceptance from the baby—someone they can love who will love them back
- rejection of family values
- a goal of revenge against parents
- a wish to get away from a difficult family life

This problem belongs to the baby's mother and father. You need to examine your feelings, the family relationship, and the situation at hand. As parents of the baby's mother, you may feel shocked or reject your daughter. Perhaps you're not ready to accept the pregnancy. But rejecting your daughter will not make the pregnancy go away. Your daughter needs understanding and support—now more than ever.

You and your daughter can seek guidance from a doctor, family therapist, member of the clergy, counselor, or social service agency. Outside help can support your family at a time when thinking straight is hard. Meeting with the baby's father and his parents may be appropriate. Everyone will need to discuss the problem openly and honestly.

All parents must begin to understand and accept what has happened. Your acceptance creates an atmosphere for problem solving. Avoid saying "I told you so." Also avoid words like *should* and *must*. You need to listen to and reflect your teens' feelings. By understanding your teens' feelings about the pregnancy, you establish mutual respect. You also increase your teens' self-esteem and sense of self-worth. You and your teens together can explore alternatives about what's best for the teens and the baby.

If you are the parents of the baby's father, you need to explore his feelings and intentions. Explore alternatives, too, about how he can act responsibly and realistically. Also, be aware of increasing legal challenges involving fathers' rights. Some courts have granted custody to teen fathers long after the child's birth.

Early marriage. To many teens, marriage may seem a way to get out of the house. They may be trying to escape the supervision and controls of home. Your teen, not you, owns the problem of wanting to marry at an early age. By fighting the idea, you may make it even more attractive.

You'll need all your STEP/Teen skills. Showing respect may be hard if you believe an early marriage is not good. Yet you still need to listen to the couple's opinions. Your understanding can help the teens decide what they want. By accepting their feelings and beliefs, you increase the chances of a responsible decision.

Help the couple decide why they want to marry now. Explore alternatives with them. For example, maybe they want to be free of parental supervision. You could say, "It seems you both want more freedom. What else might help you feel more in charge of your own lives?" Help them see other ways besides marriage. By listening, understanding, and exploring alternatives, you create a loving atmosphere.

Learn More About It

When it comes to sex, there is a lot of information "out there" for parents and teens. Where do you find it?

- Many schools and community centers have pamphlets, books, and information. Clinics and public health departments do too. Bookstores and libraries have sections with books, tapes, and videos for parents and teenagers. If you give books or tapes to your teen, be sure to talk about them.

- Schools, churches, and other organizations often offer discussion groups for parents and for teenagers.

- In the case of disease, rape, or pregnancy, most phone books have crisis numbers. Look for a section called "Community Service Numbers" or "Crisis Numbers." Then look under "Crisis Intervention," "Sexual Abuse/Assault," "Social Services," or "Youth Services." In the United States, the United Way has a "First Call for Help" number listed in most phone books.

What About Drinking and Using Other Drugs?

It's no secret that teens are under a lot of pressure to use drugs. And there are plenty of different drugs to worry about!

Becoming a Virgin Again

Some teens have had sex but wish they hadn't. There is a movement among teens to put that behind them and start fresh. The teen decides to "become a virgin" again. You might have heard this called <u>second virginity</u>. A counselor at your teen's school may have information about groups that focus on keeping or getting back virginity. If you belong to a religious organization, the youth leader may know about this movement too.

How Can I Help My Teen Stay Away From Drugs?

What Is a Drug?

- Beer, wine, and hard liquor are all drugs.

- Some ingredients in cigarettes and the caffeine in coffee and soft drinks are drugs.

- Many drugs like aspirin, non-prescription sleeping pills, and pills for staying awake can easily be bought over the counter even by children younger than teenagers.

- Legal drugs prescribed by doctors are readily available to teens.

- Illegal drugs like marijuana, speed, cocaine, and synthetic drugs are part of many teen parties.

- Inhalants—things that can be breathed in, or inhaled—are also available to teens. Some teens inhale household products like glue, paint thinner, and aerosols (spray cans) to get high.

When it comes to teens and drugs, many parents are truly afraid. They know that drugs are dangerous. They also know their teens have chances to use them. Because of that, parents sometimes tend to panic about drinking and using other drugs. When that happens, parents may forget some of the best ways to help their teens. The parents mean well, but they're worried. So instead of open questions, they start to use closed ones like "You aren't using drugs, are you?" Instead of encouraging, they show that they *expect* that their teens will abuse drugs. They give orders instead of choices. They try to control rather than guide. They use punishments instead of consequences.

Keep this in mind: The best way to help teens make good choices about drugs is by using the parenting skills you have learned in this book. You can't guarantee that your teen won't use drugs. But you can do many things to help your teenager make good choices.

The skills and approaches you have learned in *Parenting Teenagers* can help you with the following:

Build your teen's self-esteem. Young people who feel good about themselves are more likely to think for themselves. They are less likely to let friends talk them into using drugs.

Guide your teen to make decisions and solve problems. Teenagers who can do this are more likely to think about the consequences of using drugs.

Encourage healthy activities. Teens can get involved in school activities such as sports, music groups, or clubs. Your place of worship probably has healthy activities they can take part in too. Community and teen centers also have activities and programs. When possible, attend your teens' activities. Be a parent volunteer.

Be informed. Many middle schools and high schools hold information nights for parents on the subject of drugs. Many also offer parent discussion groups. Attend these meetings. You will learn a lot about what's going on in your teen's school and in your community.

There are lots of volunteer opportunities where you can get to know other parents.

Many booklets have been written for parents and teenagers about drugs. The office at your teen's school may have some. You can also learn more by calling the National Clearinghouse for Alcohol and Drug Abuse. (See "Getting Help," page 148.)

Talk to your teen about drugs. Learn the facts about drugs before you do this. Don't preach, just share. Listen to your teen's ideas about drugs. If your teen thinks drugs are "no big deal," don't overreact. Ask open questions. Keep listening. Tell your teen how you feel too. Answer your teen's questions honestly.

Listen to your teen's ideas about drugs. There are many opportunities to find out what your teen thinks—invitations to parties, news events on television, portrayals of drug-using behaviors in movies and on TV. Ask for your teen's opinion. Sometimes we get just as far by respecting and listening to our teen's concerns as we do by stating our own.

Get to know the parents of your teenager's friends. This can be harder as teens get older and make friends in many different places. It's still worth the effort. Work with other parents to plan safe, fun activities that don't include drugs.

Have family rules about parties. Setting limits is okay. It's also okay to require that:

- Parties have adults there to supervise.
- The adults in charge agree not to serve alcohol or other drugs.

Watch your own drug use. Do you smoke or drink? What message are you sending your teen? Legal drugs like alcohol and medicine can be abused. You have an opportunity to show your teen responsible use through your actions.

Don't invite trouble. You invite trouble when you leave your teen alone for the weekend. Word spreads fast in a school when parents aren't home. Even a teen who doesn't want visitors may end up with a party that's out of control. You also invite trouble when you keep an open supply of beer, wine, or liquor on hand.

How Can I Tell If My Teen Is Using Drugs?

Look for big changes in your teen's behavior. Of course, changes can happen for other reasons. And with some drugs, you won't notice changes in your teen at first. You know your teen best. If you're not sure, look further.

Here are some possible signs to look for:

- **a positive view of drugs** (magazines or posters related to drugs, collections of beer cans, lots of jokes about drugs)

When a Teen Smokes

Many teens start smoking to fit in with friends. Others seek power over their parents. Smoking is addictive.

- **Maybe your teen has tried smoking but isn't a regular smoker. Talk to your teen about the consequences of smoking. Be clear that you don't want any smoking in your home.**

- **Help an addicted teen quit smoking. Look for a quit-smoking program through your doctor or the public health department. A doctor may recommend that your teen use special methods to reduce addiction, like gum or a skin patch.**

- **Don't smoke yourself. If you do, consider joining your teen in quitting.**

- **health problems** (bloodshot eyes, lack of interest in food, tired all the time, unusual mood swings, problems remembering or paying attention, slurred speech, runny nose)

- **changes in appearance** (poor grooming, sloppy dress, t-shirts or other clothes related to drugs)

- **changes in behavior** (poor schoolwork, skipping school, skipping or quitting activities, more anger and arguing, lying, stealing, cheating, keeping secrets, having a lot of money)

- **changes in friends** (letting go of old friends, making new friends you don't know, spending little time at home)

Even with some of these signs, parents may not want to accept that their teen may be using drugs. To ignore the signs, however, puts their teen in danger. Not only that, it may cause the family serious legal problems. Parents need to check their local laws regarding their responsibility if their teen uses or deals drugs.

Two signs tell you that you need to take *immediate* action:

- **possession of drugs (including alcohol)**
- **presence of drug materials or equipment (paraphernalia)**

If you see these signs, you need to search your teen's room and things. Usually you would not do that. But if you have solid reason to believe your teen is using drugs, you need to look further. Asking your teen about it probably won't help. A teen who is using drugs has decided to lie.

What If I Think My Teen Is Using Drugs?

If you find out your teen has already experimented, use it as an opportunity to talk. Make sure your teen knows that some drugs can be *deadly*—even if used only once or in small doses.

A teen's regular use of alcohol or other drugs is *drug abuse*. With drug abuse, take action. Don't expect to handle it by yourself. Ask help from a doctor, school counselor, or a leader at your place of worship. They can help you get in touch with a counselor, clinic, or treatment center. If not, call the National Drug and Alcohol Treatment Referral Service in the United States. (See "Getting Help," page 148.) Local phone books also list drug treatment agencies. Look under "Alcohol," "Drugs," or "Chemical Abuse."

Sometimes, You Need More Help

You may have used your STEP/Teen skills and still have relationship problems with your teen. Family counseling might help. Involving the whole family is usually best. But some family members—including your teen—may not want counseling. If so, you can still help your teen by seeing a counselor yourself.

You Have Taken Another Big Step

In Chapter 7, you have seen many ways to use your parenting skills and approaches. Throughout *Parenting Teenagers*, you have learned many ways to help your teenager be independent and responsible. You help by:

- showing respect for your teen and yourself
- understanding the goals of your teen's behavior
- changing the way you respond
- expecting cooperation
- encouraging your teen
- listening and talking about feelings
- giving your teen opportunities to make decisions
- setting limits and giving choices
- working together to solve problems

All of these skills and approaches take practice. Stick with it. Be patient with yourself and your teenager. When you have trouble, think again about the challenge of parenting:

- to encourage your teenager to be healthy, confident, cooperative, and independent
- to build a strong, lifelong relationship with your teenager
- to help your teenager grow to be a responsible adult

Remember Encouragement

To change yourself or your teen, remember encouragement. Nobody changes unless they feel encouraged. Here are the basics of encouragement:

- Focus on words and feelings. Listen first if you expect to be heard.
- What are the assets? Knowing strengths and assets, we can build.
- See problems in perspective and with humor.
- Focus on effort. Don't wait for perfection. (You might wait a long time!)
- Encourage yourself. It begins a process of building encouragement with your teen.

Drug Paraphernalia

Here are some materials that often go with drug use:

- **cigarette papers**
- **tweezers or clips**
- **water pipes (often glass)**
- **scales**
- **hypodermic needles (syringes)**
- **small spoons**
- **small bottles**
- **butts, seeds, leaves**
- **small plastic bags**
- **razor blades**
- **cigarette lighters**
- **glue or aerosol cans**

What's Next?

The next step is up to you! Your teen is becoming an adult—but it won't happen overnight. Maybe you thought STEP/Teen would change your teen. Now you know that others change only as you change yourself. Patience and a sense of humor can help you keep going when things seem discouraging.

For a better relationship with your teenager, set realistic goals. First, develop the courage to be imperfect. Many of us push ourselves and our teen to be perfect. Our intentions may be good. But what we get is often not what we want. Believing that mistakes help us learn will put less presssure on you and your teen. You'll feel better about yourself. And your teen may become more cooperative and self-reliant.

Set a goal to encourage not only your teen, but also yourself. Think about how you feel respected and valued. Know that you are reaching a more satisfying relationship with your teen.

The teen years are a time of challenge. Your teenager is trying new behaviors. Your teen is also building a unique identity. See moves toward independence not as rebellion but as ways of becoming unique. The relationship between teenagers and parents affects what happens during the teen years. With courage, hope, and creativity, and by focusing on encouragement and cooperation, all relationships can improve.

Getting Help

Call for more information on problems that families and teens face. Many 800 numbers change. If that happens, call 1-800-555-1212. You may ask the operator for an updated number.

IN THE UNITED STATES:

- **National Clearinghouse for Alcohol and Drug Abuse**
  1-800-729-6686 (1-800-SAY-NOTO)
  Web site: www.health.org

- **National Drug and Alcohol Treatment Referral Service**
  1-800-HELP (1-800-662-4357)

- **American Lung Association**
  1-212-315-8700 (not a free call)

- **National AIDS Hot Line**
  1-800-342-2437 (1-800-342-AIDS)
  or **1-800-344-SIDA** (Spanish)
  or **1-800-AIDS-TTY** (hearing-impaired)

- **National Runaway Switchboard**
  1-800-621-4000

- **National Domestic Violence Hot Line**
  1-800-799-SAFE (1-800-799-7233)
  or **1-800-787-3224** (TDD)

JUST FOR YOU

Look at What You've Accomplished!

Completing a parenting book or course is an accomplishment. It shows that you can look at new ideas. It shows that you're willing to help yourself grow.

- What is new, different, and good in your family right now?

- What would you like for your teenager in one, five, and ten years?

- How can your own abilities, along with the ideas in this book, help you and your teenager in the future?

Remember, thinking about what you haven't yet accomplished is easy. But it's not usually helpful. Knowing what you *have* accomplished is more important.

IN CANADA:

- **Canadian Centre for Drug Abuse**
  1-613-235-4048

- **Drug and Alcohol Registry of Treatment (DART)**
  1-800-565-8603

- **Canadian Lung Association**
  1-613-747-6776

- **Health Canada: AIDS Community Action Program**
  1-416-392-2437

- **Missing Children Society of Canada**
  1-800-661-6160

- **National Clearinghouse for Domestic Violence**
  1-800-267-1291

Encouragement
STEP

Focus on your teen's feelings. Work to understand the feelings as fully as you can. Show that you understand. To help yourself do that:

- **Notice your teen's words, tone of voice, and actions.**

- **Think about what your teen feels and believes.**

- **Use reflective listening.**

- **Stay on your teen's topic. Respond only to what your teenager says.**

- **See the situation from your teen's point of view.**

Take the time to listen. It shows your teen that you care and want to understand.

POINTS TO REMEMBER

For Your *Family*

Keep having regular meetings. At your next meeting:

- **Talk about agreements you have made.**

- **Work together to solve problems.**

- **Make plans together.**

- **Let your teen and younger children talk. Add your ideas a little bit at a time.**

- **Have fun!**

Remember, all family members need to feel that their ideas are important.

1. The approach you use with your teen depends on what is happening.

2. To decide what to do, ask yourself who owns the problem, what the teen's goal is, what your purpose is, and how you can best help.

3. Expect all your children, teenagers and others, to get along together and solve problems among themselves.

4. If your teen lies or steals, follow through with consequences.

5. Talk openly with your teen about the choices and consequences involved with sex.

6. Alcohol, cigarettes, drug-store pills, medicines, inhalants, and illegal substances are all drugs.

7. To help your teen make good choices about drugs:

   - Build your teen's self-esteem.
   - Guide your teen to make decisions and solve problems.
   - Encourage healthy activities.
   - Be informed.
   - Talk to your teen about drugs.
   - Get to know other parents.
   - Have family rules about parties.
   - Watch your own drug use.
   - Don't invite trouble.

8. You can't guarantee your teen's safety. But you can use your parenting skills to help your teenager avoid serious problems and make good choices.

Chart 7   CHAPTER SEVEN   151

STEPS FOR DECIDING WHAT TO DO

1. **Identify the Goal of Misbehavior**

   Notice three clues:
   - how you feel
   - what you do
   - how your teen responds

2. **Decide Who Owns the Problem**

   Ask yourself:
   - Are my rights being disrespected?
   - Could anybody get hurt?
   - Is someone's property threatened?
   - Is my teen unable to take responsibility for this problem?

3. **Look at Your Purpose**

   Ask yourself:
   - Do I want to give attention? Or help my teen be self-reliant?
   - Do I want to show who's the boss? Or help my teen be independent and responsible?
   - Do I want to get even? Or show that I understand?
   - Do I want to let my teen off the hook? Or help my teen be self-confident?

4. **Choose an Approach**

   Do one, or combine approaches:
   - Ignore the misbehavior if that will help your teen cooperate.
   - Use reflective listening.
   - Use I-messages to tell how you feel.
   - Don't punish. Offer choices and let your teen learn from the consequences.
   - Explore alternatives.

5. **Keep Encouraging Your Teen and Yourself**

   To help your teen:
   - Encourage rather than praise.
   - Love and accept your teen.
   - Have faith in your teen.
   - Appreciate your teen.
   - Notice when your teen tries or improves.

   To help yourself:
   - Have patience with yourself.
   - Remember that your teen is not you.
   - Set realistic goals.
   - Use positive self-talk.
   - Be as healthy as you can.
   - Have a sense of humor.
   - Have the courage to be imperfect.

   To help your family:
   - Treat each other with respect.
   - Expect cooperation.
   - Use family meetings to solve problems and have fun.

INDEX